Fern Britton

Fern Britton

The Amazing Life of TV's Brightest Star

SARAH MARSHALL

JOHN BLAKE

Published by John Blake Publishing Ltd,
3 Bramber Court, 2 Bramber Road,
London W14 9PB, England

www.blake.co.uk

First published in hardback in 2007

ISBN 978 1 84454 409 7

British Library Cataloguing-in-Publication Data:

A catalogue record for this book is available from the British Library.

Design by www.envydesign.co.uk

Printed and bound in Great Britain by Creative Print and Design,
Ebbw Vale, Wales

1 3 5 7 9 10 8 6 4 2

Papers used by John Blake Publishing are natural, recyclable products
made from wood grown in sustainable forests. The manufacturing
processes conform to the environmental regulations of the country
of origin.

Every attempt has been made to contact the relevant copyright-holders,
but some were unobtainable. We would be grateful if the appropriate
people could contact us.

To Fiona Wootton,
My Friend For Life

Contents

Chapter 1

A Taste For Theatre

At the age of five, two minutes can seem an eternity. Sitting out on the sidelines, Fern waited patiently for her name to be called. But by the time her turn came to take the floor, she felt as if an entire lifetime had whizzed past. Nervously, she stood up and took her position on the PE mat. Beads of sweat rolled down inside the back of her judo jacket as she prepared to defend herself against her opponent. She tugged at her yellow belt with pride, partly to demonstrate that she was one tough cookie who should not be messed with and partly because her oversized trousers were falling down.

As the gym teacher called for silence, a nervous tension gripped the room. Like tigers watching their prey, the two girls moved stealthily round the mat. As the adrenalin kicked in, Fern's heart started to race, pounding loudly – she was certain everyone could hear it beating. Suddenly, she felt giddy. With butterflies rising in her stomach, she felt overwhelmed and quickly gulped, swallowing back the acidic taste of sickness. Time ground to a standstill. As much as Fern enjoyed her after-school judo classes, class demonstrations were always nerve-wracking.

'Brrrriiiiiing.' A shrill ringing ripped through the room. It was the school bell. The lesson was over. 'What a shame!' called the instructor, clasping his hands. 'We'll have to stop now. It's time to go home.' Fern felt a rush of disappointment. She had built herself up into a frenzy and secretly wanted to show off her moves. But when Fern noticed a familiar face pressed up against the window in the door to the hall, her disappointment quickly subsided.

Grabbing her gym kit, she raced over to the door. 'Dad!' she screamed, flinging her arms round his neck. He had been waiting outside for the last ten minutes, proudly observing his feisty daughter in action. As a working actor, estranged from his wife, Tony Britton rarely had time to spend with his daughter. Subsequently he treasured every moment. Collecting Fern from her judo lesson remains one of his most vivid memories as a parent.

'She was in full judo kit with a fearsome-looking yellow belt around her waist and she was exactly as she is now, so full of fun and vitality,' he fondly recalled. 'I didn't know quite how to deal with it. Whatever a child does, you have to encourage them. So I felt I should say, "Well done, come and knock me over."'

Fern Britton was born on 17 July 1957 in Ealing in west London to Ruth and Tony Britton. She had one sister called Cherry, who was eight years her senior. Born in Birmingham in 1924, Tony was a successful film, theatre and television actor. These days he is probably most famous for his role alongside Nigel Havers and Dinah Sheridan, as Dr Toby Latimer in the popular eighties BBC sitcom *Don't Wait Up*. But success came at a price. Tony's heavy workload often meant that he had little time to spend with his family. He would frequently leave home early in the morning, returning long after the girls had been put to bed. Every night, he would sneak in to give his two little angels a kiss goodnight. Gently easing the door open, he would tiptoe quietly into the room so as not to disturb their peaceful slumber. Occasionally, Fern would stir, opening her eyes for a split second, mumble something incomprehensible, roll over and sink straight back into sleep. 'That's my girl,' Tony would smile to himself.

But as time went on, Fern saw less and less of her father. His workload placed an intolerable strain on his marriage to Ruth and the couple would often bicker. Eventually, they decided it would be best for everyone if they parted ways and pursued separate lives. By the time Fern was five years old, her parents had divorced. Thankfully, the split was amicable and left few scars on the impressionable child. Ruth took care of the children, while Tony visited whenever possible. Unfortunately, this proved to be easier said than done as Tony's career took a sharp upturn. 'I have no memories of my father being at home,' recalled Fern. 'Just of him working and, as a special treat, being allowed to see him in the theatre.' As a member of the Royal Shakespeare Company he was involved in several prestigious productions, such as *A Midsummer Night's Dream* (1954, George Devin) and much later, *Twelfth Night* (1994, Ian Judge) and *Henry V* (1995, Matthew Warchus). Ruth kept his make-up box and would bring it out for the girls whenever they showed signs of missing their father. Fern would gleefully rifle through the box, pulling out odds and ends for closer examination. Tony's collection of fake beards never ceased to amaze her. To her sister Cherry's amusement, Fern would hold them up to her face, making impressions of a gruff old man. When her mother was not looking, she would unseal the powder cases and, using a sweaty digit, would daub make-up all over her face. An intoxicating smell of greasepaint flooded the room. Even today, Fern can close her eyes and conjure up that same smell. Some children recall their father's aftershave, but Fern would forever remember the waft of stage make-up. 'That was the first experience of my father,' she grinned. 'Through scent and touch.'

During the sixties, Tony also appeared in several

television dramas. Aware that it was important for the girls to have a good relationship with their father, Ruth always allowed Cherry and Fern to watch the shows. Whenever Tony appeared on screen, Fern would jump up and lunge towards the television set. She would wave frantically, hoping to grab his attention. When he failed to respond, her smile would slump into a frown. Baffled, she turned to Ruth. 'Mummy, why doesn't Daddy wave?' she complained.

A similar situation occurred whenever Fern went to see her father perform at the theatre. At any point when he looked directly towards the audience, she would leap up and wave. Only this time she realized that Tony could not wave back. A well-behaved child, she refrained from actually calling out his name and disrupting the show. Mummy had told her it was fine to wave, but she had to remain quiet. 'I never understood what the plays were about,' admitted Fern. 'But I would sit very quietly and wave. I realised that he couldn't wave back because he was acting.'

Although many of the highbrow performances blurred into one, Fern distinctly remembered a trip to see her father in the stage version of *My Fair Lady*. She was just seven years old at the time. There was one scene in particular that upset the young Fern. 'I thought that he was incredibly rude to Eliza when he said that she was a squashed cabbage leaf. To me, it seemed so unfair because she was obviously such a nice girl.'

After the show, Fern angrily confronted her father. Stamping her feet, she demanded to know why he had been so mean. Laughing, Tony scooped the little girl up into his arms and planted a kiss on her head. He explained that it was all part of the script and that he had been acting out a role. Fern was amazed by the powers of such make-believe. From that moment on began a love affair with the theatre that would extend well into her adult years.

Although Tony was rarely around, Fern never felt a distinct sense of loss. She was too young really to understand what was happening and Ruth did a fantastic job of making home life fun. 'I had never known him to be there in the first place!' shrugged Fern. She describes her father as 'an heroic, distant figure... My father was a very glamorous figure who was always away on tour or appearing in the West End. So we didn't see much of him when we were growing up, although we were always in touch.'

Despite the fact they were no longer together, Ruth held no bitter feelings towards her estranged husband. In fact, she was extremely proud of him. If ever she walked past a newsstand and spied a magazine featuring his name, she would always buy it. After every new show, she would sift through the newspapers and save any reviews, sticking the press cuttings into several scrapbooks. Years later, Fern and Cherry would beg to look through them.

The couple had been married for ten extremely happy

years and Ruth wasn't about to dismiss those memories overnight. Besides, it was important for the girls to remember that their father still loved them very much. At first Fern could not understand why her parents were spending more and more time apart, but sensitive to changes in emotion she soon gauged exactly what was going on. Especially when Tony remarried and it became apparent that he had a new family to care for as well. Fern later found herself with a stepbrother, Jasper. 'Somehow, as a little girl, I knew instinctively that my parents didn't get on any more,' she said. 'I knew that my father had a new family and I accepted that. We were happy in our situation and we knew that he was happy in his.'

To her credit, Ruth did a great job of giving her children a smooth ride. But behind the scenes, life was not so rosy. Around the time of her divorce, Ruth's mother suffered a stroke. At one point it seemed as if the whole world was caving in on her, but she refused to give in. Making Cherry and Fern her focus, she held her head high and struggled onwards. Looking back, Fern has only admiration for her mother, whom she fondly refers to as Addie. 'My mother coped brilliantly with bringing us up,' she gushed. 'Of course, I now realise that there were a lot of painful areas that were never mentioned.'

Indeed, there were instances when Ruth would break down in tears. 'We did have quite a bumpy childhood because my mother had quite a rough time,' Fern sympathised. 'Life was not easy for her.' But the tight-knit trio muddled through: 'There were some difficult times, but they weren't insurmountable.'

Weathering every emotional storm that came her way, Ruth remained admirably calm. 'I never remember my mother looking even mildly stressed,' gasped Fern. 'And she never moaned about anything. She never had a bad word to say about my father.'

Although Ruth never asked her children to choose sides, Fern admits to having a closer relationship with her mother. Fern would do anything to make her mother smile. Like most single-parent families, Ruth and her two girls were prone to financial hardships. Christmas was particularly tough. Ruth cut back on her little luxuries such as cosmetics and beauty products, in a bid to care for her children. Returning the favour, Fern saved for weeks to buy her mother a present. Aware that her mother was feeling low, she wanted to buy something that would make her feel better. 'I'd save for weeks to even afford my mother a face cream!' recalled Fern. 'But I think a bit of struggling is no bad thing. It makes each present mean more, each memory last longer.' When Fern did finally present her mother with the gift, Ruth was overwhelmed with emotion. She was touched that Fern understood the sacrifices a mother was forced to make.

Fern learned a lot from her mother and is forever indebted to her for being such a wonderful role model. When Fern faced her own difficulties much later in adult life, she turned to her mother for advice and inspiration. 'My mother taught me never to be beaten,' she proudly declared. 'When things are bad, she taught us that it will get better.'

But strength of will was not the only quality Fern inherited from her mother. Ruth also passed on some more unconventional talents to both her daughters. 'My sister is psychic and so is my mother,' Fern revealed. As a child, Fern had her own fair share of premonitions, although she found the whole experience quite alarming. She recalls several vivid dreams. Each time she would wake up in a sweat, alarmed by their content. 'When I was little, I had two or three premonitions of friends and family dying, and then they did in the circumstances I dreamed,' she recalled with a shudder. 'That frightened me, so I had to stop.'

Despite her reluctance to participate in paranormal activities, Fern is anything but a sceptic. She was brought up in a Christian household and has always been interested in exploring spiritual beliefs. A regular churchgoer she was even confirmed. As a young adult, she would regularly attend discussion groups with her rector. But she was also receptive to new-age philosophies, and wore a quartz crystal around her neck.

Although, for the most part, Fern appeared to be a stable child, Ruth constantly worried about her wellbeing. Occasionally, she over-compensated for Tony's absence by monitoring her daughter too closely. When

Fern ate very little at meal times, Ruth grew extremely concerned. Her daughter was already on the skinny side. She had read numerous articles about unhappy children refusing to eat, but until the age of five, Fern refused to finish her meals. Twirling her fork, she would playfully rearrange the food on her plate to make pretty pictures. Unfortunately, more food ended up on the tablecloth than in her mouth. 'I didn't like eating,' claimed Fern.

Every day, Ruth would try and encourage Fern to eat more food. Sometimes, she did not even let the poor child leave the table until her plate was completely clean. Brussels sprouts, carrots, potatoes... nothing was left to waste. Bizarrely, the only thing Fern did hanker after were lamb bones. After every Sunday lunch, she scoured the dinner plates for any leftover scraps. Collecting together her finds, she would crawl under the kitchen table and, closing her eyes, she would savour every mouthful. 'I would suck out the marrow, like a little dog!' she laughed.

These were the beginnings of Fern's love affair with food. Little did Ruth know that weight issues would later dominate Fern's life. 'I was encouraged to eat,' remembered Fern. Each time the young child cleared her plate, Ruth would give her a reassuring pat on the head. 'Ooh, good!' she cooed. 'Look at your tummy coming on. That's great!' By the time Fern was nine years old, she was starting to put on weight. Her cheeks filled out and her complexion took on a new healthy glow.

Admittedly, Fern was fortunate to grow up surrounded

by talent. Her stepbrother Jasper would eventually grow up to be an actor. One day, Tony took him to visit Shakespeare's grave. Little did Jasper know that in a few years' time he would be following in his father's footsteps by joining the Royal Shakespeare Company. While Fern's sister Cherry would grow up to be an author. But as a child, Fern often felt like the underachiever. She constantly played down her talents, describing her abilities as average. 'Everyone in my family was so successful,' she complained. 'They were always the ones who were going to be brilliant, not me.' Not everyone would agree with her. Casting her mind back, Cherry can identify several early indications of her little sister's eventual rise to fame: 'I always knew she'd be a star when, aged seven, she won the reading cup at school. She was always very bright, a good storyteller, very funny and I love her very much.'

On the morning of the presentation, Fern was extremely nervous. Her teachers were holding a special end-of-term presentation ceremony, where all the high-achieving students were to be honoured with rewards. Fern had always been good at writing stories. She had a vivid imagination and would often regale her parents with fantastical tales. It came as no surprise, then, that she should be rewarded for her talents. Ruth picked out a special outfit for her daughter to wear. Everyone gathered in the school hall and when Fern's name was called, Tony and Ruth clapped and cheered enthusiastically. Their encouragement made Fern blush. Tugging nervously at her waistband, she walked up to collect her award. Too embarrassed to stay on stage for long, she scuttled back to her seat. Once the family clan reached home, she was treated to a special family dinner, and Ruth promised to frame her certificate and give it pride of place on the wall.

But writing stories was not the only thing Fern proved to be good at – she was actually pretty adept at acting them out. Tony noticed his daughter's talent from a young age. Weaned on theatre productions, it was hardly surprising that she should develop a taste of her own for acting. She seized eagerly on the opportunity to perform in school plays. Often her parts were minor, but she relished every moment on stage. She recalled taking part in a performance of *Rag, Tag and Bobtail* at the age of six. 'We were little pixies, painting the chestnut buds with sticky stuff,' said Fern, smiling at the memory. For weeks she practised dancing with her brush, determined to make her movements look as realistic as possible. She loved spinning round in her pixie outfit and often begged Ruth to let her wear it all evening, even after rehearsals had finished.

The final show took place in the village hall. Backstage, Fern could hear the seats filling up out front. 'Now, none of you are to go outside before the show begins,' demanded her teacher. The cast of small children nodded obediently. But Fern could not help herself. She was dying to see how many people had actually turned up. When her teacher's back was turned, she crept forwards and took a peek through the red velvet stage curtains. She gasped. Nearly every seat was already taken and with ten minutes to show-time, people were still arriving. At the back of the room, another teacher was frantically arranging additional makeshift seating. Fern scanned the room for any familiar faces. She instantly spotted Ruth and her sister, Cherry. But her smile broke into a huge beam when she noticed who was sitting beside them – her father, Tony. Although she rarely saw him these days, he always made a special effort to attend school plays. Forgetting her teacher's instructions, she waved, desperately trying to grab Daddy's attention. Recognising the small, chubby arm protruding from the curtain, Tony smiled and waved back. 'Darling,' he whispered, 'remember – you can only wave when you're in the audience, but not up on stage!' Eager to please, Fern quickly scuttled off to find her magic paintbrush.

She waited patiently in the wings for her on-stage cue. Even though she had practised the scene a million times, Fern was still convinced that she might mess things up. She counted down the seconds, her heart pounding in the back of her throat. Suddenly her time was up. She glided onto the stage in pursuit of her fellow pixies. Things were going well. But then she turned to face the audience and lost her concentration. She heard a smashing sound as her glue pot hit the floor. For a moment, Fern stood paralysed with fear, but seconds later her reflexes kicked in. 'As we were under strict instructions to keep on acting no matter what happened, I mimed the pot.' Unfortunately, Fern was not completely out of the woods. Even though her first little mishap had largely passed by unnoticed, it was not quite so easy to pull it off a second time around. 'I dropped the brush!' she says, still cringing some forty-odd years later. But a true professional, she carried on and mimed the brush. All she could think of, however, was what her father might think: 'I was panic-stricken, thinking, "Oh my God, he's out there."' Thankfully, Tony was more than understanding. After the show, he gave Fern an enormous hug and commended her initiative. A lesser actor would have buckled in a similar situation, he told her. After all, improvisation was the key to true acting talent.

Like most fathers, Tony would forever remember his little princess as a small girl. 'Fern's personality was all there,' he smiled, misty eyed. 'Even as a toddler, she was very bright, independent and unselfish – I think you're born with those sorts of character traits.' But inevitably, Fern grew up. Almost overnight, she became a young woman. Fern recalled how a number of physical changes took place: 'The summer I was fourteen something happened. All the hormones kicked in. I grew a bit, lost weight, bosoms arrived and I became quite shapely.'

During her teenage years, Fern forged a closer connection with her absentee father. Now a little older, she understood why his visits had been so infrequent during her childhood. They did not necessarily mean that he loved her any the less. Divorce was simply a reality of life. At the time, Fern was attending Dr Challoner's School in Little Chalfont, Buckinghamshire. She had even less opportunity to see her father, so started writing him letters.

'I was grown up with new freedoms and I got in touch and we started seeing more of each other,' recalled Fern. 'When you're older you suddenly see your parents as fallible people and a stronger bond forms. You become friends and not just parent and child.'

Tony was flattered that his daughter had taken the time to put pen to paper and always eagerly awaited her correspondence. Without fail, he always wrote in return. 'I loved getting his amusing, affectionate letters back,' she smiles.

Daddy's little girl was clearly turning into a mature woman.

To her credit, Ruth encouraged Fern to contact her father. Even though she had largely brought up Fern and Cherry as a single parent, she bore no resentment to Tony. All she ever had were kind words. Fern was relieved that she would never have to choose between her parents. 'There were never any problems,' she grinned. 'My mother is a sensational and quite unusual woman and she made it calm for all of us and never jeopardised my relationship with my father in any way. I never heard a bad word about either of them from either camp. I had a very happy childhood.'

Fern was extremely proud of her father's achievements. 'When I was seventeen, my English teacher was arranging a theatre trip and I said I'd like to see my father in the *Dame of Sark*,' she recalled. 'So we went off in a minibus and twelve of us went backstage to see him afterwards.' Tony greeted Fern with a hug. He was more than happy to show her friends around the theatre and extremely gratified that they had chosen to come and see his play. Fern was equally proud. 'That was wonderful because it was the first time I was able to show him off in front of my contemporaries. I was so proud of him.'

Over time, Fern began to idolise her father. Removed from her everyday life, he became some sort of mystical figure. 'Dad never disciplined me and, as we only saw the best side of each other, he was almost a fantasy figure. All I ever saw was the perfectly-groomed end product, so that was a hard act for other men to follow.' In fact, Fern would use her father as a benchmark for any prospective suitors. Unfortunately, most fell short of her expectations: 'He [Tony] was extremely suave and charming, and few young men had the same sophistication.'

Fortunately, Fern had more important issues on her mind. With age came ambition. Fern started to think about her future, wondering what she would like to do for the rest of her life. Admittedly, she never had great aspirations. But she always dreamed of doing something that made her happy. Work in the theatre was an obvious choice. It was all she had ever really loved. Tony was more than happy to help his daughter get her foot on the first rung of the ladder. He eagerly organised an application for her to go to the Central School of Drama. But, to his surprise, Fern had few aspirations of becoming an actress. 'I was staggered when I saw that she had put down that she wanted to be a stage manager rather than an actress,' said Tony, who was aghast at the time. 'Because of her personality and beauty, I assumed that she would want to act.'

Fern had other ideas. The limelight held little appeal for her. She much preferred working behind the scenes. 'After I finished my A-levels I became a stage manager and I loved every minute of it!' she explained. All the cast and crew she worked with had only kind words to say about Fern. She had an unshakeable resolve and brought a wonderful sense of calm to even the most stressful of situations. 'Fern is the most well-organised person I know!' gushed her father, Tony. 'Which was a gift when she was a stage manager.' While actors fussed and flustered around her, she refused to be drawn into a panic.

One particularly amusing incident involving a corkscrew sticks in Fern's mind. During a scene, one of the actors was required to open a bottle of wine. For some reason, they seemed to be having incredible difficulty with such a simple task. Fern had already purchased several different types of foolproof corkscrew in a bid to make life easier. But the actor was still having problems.

'Darling, I can't possibly open this bottle of wine in

scene three,' complained the troubled thespian. 'How do I know it will work?'

Sympathetic to her colleague's needs, Fern refrained from laughing. Instead, she took the matter in hand. 'Don't worry,' she smiled, 'we'll practise a few times first. In case of emergency, I'll have a bottle already opened.'

'She is very maternal,' said Tony. 'If she were an animal, she would be a sheepdog rounding people up. The moment actors go into a theatre, they go stupid. It was very easy for Fern to be mummy and say, "Now, darling, of course you can, how would you like me to lay this out for you?"' In short, Fern made life as easy, painless and enjoyable as possible for anyone who crossed her path. From very early on, she had a reputation for saving the day.

Even though Tony was all too aware of the pitfalls involved in a career in the theatre, he did little to deter his daughter from following suit. 'Even people in the business asked me if I'd find it difficult to let my children go on the stage,' admitted Tony. He would always reply 'no' and query their concern. 'But it's such a tough business!' came the common response. Tony simply smiled. He had no concerns. Sure the theatre was a tough business, but Fern was an even tougher cookie. He had no doubts that she would exceed all expectations: 'I was lucky enough to know that whatever Fern wanted to do, she would be all right, she would be able to do it. It was always obvious to me that Fern was going to be successful at something, whatever it turned out to be.'

Success, however, did not arrive overnight. Wages in the theatre business were notoriously low and Fern spent her early twenties struggling to make ends meet. In truth, it was not too much of a shock to the system. There had been times during her childhood when finances had been low and she had become accustomed to sacrificing luxuries and honestly did not mind doing without new clothes and beauty products. But that did not make thrifty living any less of a challenge. 'When I was a single woman in my twenties, I was really broke!' she exclaimed. 'I remember having only 23p!' Refusing to be beaten, Fern conjured up all sorts of ingenious methods to save money. When she grew really desperate, she even admitted in a *TV Times* interview to stealing pints of milk and newspapers from the theatre office! Feeling slightly guilty, she appeased her conscience by convincing herself that it was all payment in kind for the hours of overtime she had put in.

From an early age, Fern had set her priorities in place. She desperately loved her work and that more than made up for a limited wardrobe! But, most importantly of all, she was surrounded by close friends and family. No amount of money could buy that sort of happiness. During her twenties, Fern made the most of the new relationship that she had successfully forged with her father. They would meet up regularly and attend shows or visit new restaurants.

'My father likes to eat well and he introduced me to some really good restaurants,' smiled Fern. Fern always listened intently as Tony ran through the menu. He often knew the chefs by name and could recommend all the best dishes. The pair would chat animatedly for hours, making up for lost time. Some people even mistakenly took Fern for Tony's younger girlfriend! The idea of Tony being her sugar daddy amused Fern immensely. She took great pleasure in loudly addressing him as 'Dad'. 'Dining together, we did get a few strange looks, the odd raised eyebrow,' smirked Fern. 'Look at that man with a woman half his age… I took great pleasure in making it perfectly clear that, actually, he was my father.'

On several occasions, the pair even took off on holiday together. A well-cultured man, Tony relished any opportunity to give guided tours. Whether it was kicking back on the beach or wandering round church ruins, Fern enjoyed every minute of his company. She could even forgive him for the long country walks that he made her take in sub-zero temperatures! As he told her time and time again, fresh air was good for the soul! Conscious that he had missed out on his little girl growing up, Tony was determined not to let any future opportunities slip through his fingers. But Fern did not hold a grudge: she understood that the situation had been difficult for her father and was touched by the amount of effort he was now investing in their relationship. 'It was great catching up on all the things I never did with him when I was little,' she said fondly.

Unfortunately, there was a downside to the number of

gourmet dinners that Fern and Tony enjoyed. Fern developed a taste for rich foods and could rarely resist a dessert. In marked contrast to a childhood spent skipping meals, Fern had now developed a healthy appetite. As Tony piled on the dinner invitations, Fern started to pile on the pounds. By her mid-twenties, the characteristically confident young women developed an uncharacteristic obsession with her body weight. Looking back, Fern describes herself as 'unhealthily body-focused'. All of a sudden her jeans felt tighter and she often had to yank on the top button just to do them up. 'I'd start to think, "God, I'm ten and a half stone. I used to be eight and a half stone," and all that,' she shuddered. Growing increasingly concerned, she would pass up on creamy dishes and desserts, all the time eyeing up her father's choices. It was torturous. Tony noticed something was up and chastised his daughter for being so ridiculous. As far as he was concerned, she had a fantastic figure. Why on earth did she want to look like a carbon copy of all those stick-thin skeletons on television?

Fern would respond with a sigh of resignation. She knew he was right. 'Actually, I was quite normal,' she says now, flicking through old photographs. 'Size ten is too thin for me, I'm not that shape.' But Fern persisted in losing a few pounds. She did not want to go overboard, but it was time to start thinking sensibly about her diet. Exercising a bit of willpower, she managed to drop back to a size fourteen. 'That was much better for me,' she recalled. 'I meandered between nine and a half and ten and a half stone.'

Everyone congratulated Fern on losing weight. She had worked hard. Unfortunately, not everyone was quite so complementary about her new body shape. After several years of working in the theatre, Fern decided it was time for a new challenge. She spent a few months mulling over her different career options. She was not hugely ambitious, but simply wanted to work with fun and inspirational people. A creative environment tended to suit her best, so she decided to stick within that realm. With little inclination to become an actress, she felt it was time to take a break from the theatre. One friend suggested that she should investigate working in television. At first, Fern simply nodded in agreement, only half seriously considering the suggestion. But after some thought, it dawned on her that a career on the small screen was actually a really appealing idea. She started scouting for presenting positions and stumbled upon a vacancy at Westward Television: 'I wanted to train dolphins, or be a nurse, or a policewoman.' So Fern sent in a show reel and was called back for a screen test. Even after five minutes, Fern had a good feeling about the job. Nodding and whispering to each other, the producers seemed suitably impressed. Fortunately, Fern's hunch had been right and a few days later she received a call confirming that the job was all hers.

Fern was over the moon. She instantly rang Tony to

share her good news and he was equally ecstatic. Even today, Fern puts her big break down to good fortune. With so many young women desperate for a career in television, she could not believe that she had actually made it. Surely they deserved the job more than she did! 'I can't believe I haven't been found out!' she exclaimed. 'I've never been ambitious.'

Fern arrived promptly for her first day of work, wanting to impress her new bosses. Unfortunately, a trip to wardrobe spelled the end of her good mood. Fern was given a selection of outfits to wear on television. In a jubilant mood, she cracked a few jokes about which colour matched her complexion, but while sifting through the clothing rail, she noticed the wardrobe assistant was staring intently at her. Fern suddenly felt self-conscious.

'What's the matter?' she asked. Had she spilt ketchup down her blouse or something?

'Hmmm,' sighed the assistant. 'The arms could be a problem,' she continued to mutter under her breath.

'What do you mean?' said Fern, examining her upper torso with concern.

'You must *never* wear anything sleeveless,' instructed the assistant.

'Why?' asked a baffled Fern.

'Because of your footballer's shoulders!' came the cruel reply.

Fern was shocked. This wasn't quite the 'dressing down' she had expected in wardrobe. A little hurt, she turned away and composed herself. She imagined what her father might advise in this situation. 'Laugh it off, girl!' he would say. So that is exactly what Fern did. However, this was just the first of many cruel jibes Fern would encounter. 'Welcome to the world of television,' she thought to herself. 'That did it,' she recalled. 'From then on, I had at least fifteen years of trauma about the tops of my arms.'

Determined to prove her critics wrong, the defiant presenter embarked on an exercise course. But she refused to cave in and adopt a ridiculous dieting regime. It would take more than a silly comment to make her give up those tasty gourmet dinners!

Thankfully, that first unfortunate encounter did not throw Fern off course. Soon those unkind words became a minor blip on the horizon, and overall, Fern loved her new job. Over time her profile began to grow. Very soon, her fame would outweigh even her father's. 'When I used to go down to see her at Westward TV, people in the street would recognise me and say, "You're Fern Britton's dad",' said Tony incredulously. 'It's gone on like that ever since.'

In 1982, Fern worked for the BBC as a senior presenter with *Spotlight South West* and then moved on to BBC1's *Breakfast Time* and *News Afternoon*. She even made the history books by becoming the youngest-ever national news presenter. Her talents did not go unnoticed. Television bosses were suitably impressed by her friendly and approachable manner and the public loved tuning in to watch her read the news. Many found her manner extremely soothing.

But the job was not without its sacrifices. As an early morning television presenter, Fern kissed goodbye to her social life. Having to rise at the crack of dawn, she would go to bed early every night. At first, she tried to burn the candle at both ends, but quickly realised that would not be possible. The demands of her job were intense and she had to be on the ball. The erratic schedule also interfered with her body clock and subsequently she put on weight. 'I am prone to putting on weight,' she admitted. 'It's very boring and it's very upsetting, but I have developed a philosophy about it over the years. I'm an ordinary woman and I actually think people appreciate the fact you've got a spot, greasy hair and have put on half a stone – perhaps half of the female population have, too!'

In spite of her weight concerns, Fern Britton was an instant hit. Both the television bosses and the viewing public clearly recognised her talents. She had that magical star quality which few presenters possess. Although the young hopeful was merely starting out on her career path, it was obvious that a long road lay ahead of her. Very soon, she was flooded with job offers. But that was not the only proposal awaiting her. Marriage was also on the cards.

Chapter 2

Ups and Downs and Early Motherhood

The south coast broadcasting station TVS was just one of the many television channels interested in recruiting Fern. TVS was the broadcasting name associated with the ITV franchise holder in the south and southeast of England at the time and until 1992. It was 1984 and Greg Dyke, the new managing director, was determined that she should join the team. He gave the challenge of recruiting her to a young, ambitious colleague called Clive Jones. Clive was already an extremely successful figure in the industry, with past employers including Yorkshire Television and TV-AM. He would later go on to become executive producer at Carlton. It was his job to try and convince Fern that she should come and work for the company.

He put in a call to her agent and suggested that she come in for an interview.

Although Clive had seen Fern on television, nothing could prepare him for meeting her in the flesh. He was bowled over by her beauty and charm. It was her smile that really caught him. The pair sat down and discussed Fern's past work and her prospective future with the company. Greg had been right – securing her services would be an industry coup. As the interview progressed, the pair realised that they had a lot more than their career focus in common. They both agreed to meet up, should Fern take the job.

Fortunately for Clive, Fern was suitable impressed and accepted a job with TVS in 1985, which necessitated a move to Southampton. She had grown accustomed to living on the coast and was relieved to be living in another maritime area. The TVS studio overlooked the water and afforded fantastic views of the boats sailing into harbour. She loved her new job as a senior presenter with the nightly news magazine *Coast to Coast* and quickly made friends with her new work colleagues, including Fred Dineage. Their partnership was so successful that the pair went on to co-present the lunchtime spin-off series *Coast to Coast People* in 1987. The content featured interviews with both famous people and local celebrities. While at TVS, Fern also co-presented the networked *Airport 90* programmes with Nick Owen and *Magic Moments*. In 1989, she presented the *Gloria Hunniford Show* on BBC Radio Two while Gloria was on holiday.

Professionally, life could not have been better for Fern. Her personal life had also taken an upturn. From the moment they met, Clive Jones had been smitten with Fern. He had that gut feeling any person can instantly recognise as love. Fern had enjoyed his company, but thought nothing more of it. For starters, she had a whole new career to think about! But just as Greg Dyke had been determined that Fern should not slip through their fingers, Clive knew that this was the fish that could not get away. Confused, he did not know what to do next. Fortunately, advice was on hand from none other than Sir David Frost! The pair had arranged a luncheon engagement and, during the meal, Clive unburdened himself and spoke of his dilemma. David smiled. He knew exactly what Clive should do.

It was all the reassurance the love-struck suitor required. After lunch, the pair shook hands and Clive hailed a taxi. 'Hatton Garden!' he called to the driver. He was heading straight to London's prestigious jewellery quarter and home to the United Kingdom's diamond centre. Clive was on his way to purchase an engagement ring. During lunch, he had reached the conclusion that he wanted Fern to be his wife. He had never been surer about something in his entire life.

Clive could not wait to present Fern with the ring. It was a beautiful sparkler and had set him back a small fortune. But it did not matter. Fern was worth it. He spent hours trying to pick the most opportune moment to propose, but something always came up. In the end, he simply decided to go for broke. Going down on one knee, he looked up at Fern and asked her to be his wife. Clasping her hand over her mouth, she gasped with surprise. She did not know what to say. Clive's proposal was completely unexpected... but that did not mean to say that it was unwelcome. Giving the matter a minute's thought, Fern nodded her head and said yes.

With a great career ahead of her and a new husband, life could not have been better for Fern. But Fern could hardly rest on her laurels. When the TVS franchise was handed over to Meridian in 1992, Fern was forced to seek alternative employment. As a parting gesture to the network, Fern and her colleague Fred presented a special programme *Goodbye To All That* looking back at high points in the history of TVS. Fred went on to present the replacement television show *Meridian Tonight*. Fern, however, chose not to follow him. She decided that her stint at TVS had run its natural course and that it was time to move on. She was beginning to miss the bright lights of London and decided it was time to return home. Given her growing reputation in the industry, it was not too hard to find a job. It just so happened that the nightly news and entertainment programme *London Tonight* was looking for an entertainment correspondent and Fern fitted the bill perfectly. She and Clive packed up their belongings and moved back to the Big Smoke.

As it turned out, 1993 would be the year of Fern Britton's life: she had a new job, a fabulous new home and best of all she gave birth to twins – Harry and Jack! 'It was the year of my life,' she said, looking back. 'Nothing could top it.' At thirty-six years of age, Fern was relatively old to be having children. 'I did want children in my twenties,' she admitted. 'But I hadn't found the right person.' But at least age brought with it wisdom. As a mature adult, she felt more than capable of rearing a family. She had taken her fair share of holidays and been to more social gatherings than she could remember. Now it was time to settle down and bring up a family. Despite the upheavals of divorce, her own parents had done a great job and Fern was determined to follow in their footsteps. 'Personally I don't think I would have been grown-up enough before,' she reasoned at the time. 'Fate has dealt me this hand and, fortunately, I have enjoyed going along with it.'

After working on *London Tonight*, Fern moved over to ITV's flagship breakfast show *GMTV* in 1999. She had landed herself a regular presenting slot on the 'Top Of The Morning' feature. Ironically, she was not the only *GMTV* presenter to fall pregnant. Scottish presenter Lorraine Kelly had announced that she was also expecting her first baby in the summer. Lorraine and Fern had become close friends on the show and, just like Fern,

Lorraine had a loyal following among the viewers. During their pregnancies, both women would share tips with each other. Fern made several jokes about the fact they had both conceived at roughly the same time. 'There must be something about that sofa at *GMTV*,' she laughed. 'Everyone who sits on it seems to get pregnant.'

Fern carried on working for the show, but twenty-eight weeks into her pregnancy she told her television bosses that it was time for her to take maternity leave. While she had managed to battle through the morning sickness, general fatigue eventually set in. The early morning starts were exhausting. Often Fern would arrive at work feeling completely wiped out. There were even several moments where she almost passed out! She would suddenly feel extremely hot under the studio lights and would reach for a glass of water to calm herself down. An ultra-scan showed that she was expecting twins, which put an even greater strain on her body. Clive grew increasingly concerned about his wife's welfare and suggested that she should take better care of herself. Fern agreed with him whole-heartedly. She loved her work, but family had always been her priority. She was willing to sacrifice her work for the good of her unborn sons. 'Mentally, I was fine, but physically I began to feel uncomfortable and rather faint,' she explained. 'I was a liability and with a show like that you can't ring up and say you're not feeling up to going in that day.'

Unfortunately for Fern, the pregnancy did not run

completely smoothly. Late into her pregnancy, Fern began to experience several unusual pains. Alarmed by their frequency, she thought that there must be something wrong and made an emergency appointment with her doctor. After several tests, the doctor informed her that she had a fibroid. 'It's a horrible, lumpy, benign tumour,' she explained. 'Very often, it's inside the womb, but mine was on the outside.'

Statistics show that about 25 per cent of white women and 50 per cent of black women suffer from fibroids during their reproductive years. Fern happened to be one of those unlucky few. At first, she panicked, but with reassurance from her doctor she realised her unborn babies would be safe. But nothing could prepare Fern for the sudden bouts of unpredictable and excruciating pain. 'The pain was tremendous,' she shuddered. 'I would be perfectly fine one minute, then the pain would go from zero to one hundred in five seconds. It was terrible!'

During those moments, Clive could do little to console his distraught wife, except mop her brow and promise her that everything was going to be fine. Taking deep breaths, Fern would try desperately hard to compose herself. After a few minutes, the pain would subside. On one occasion, however, Clive came home to find his wife crawling around the kitchen floor in agony. 'What's wrong, darling!' he cried, throwing his coat down and rushing to her side. Doubled over and wincing with pain, Fern was gasping for air. 'It's OK,' he whispered

33

reassuringly, stroking her hair. 'Just calm down and it will pass.' Thankfully, it did, but after that incident Clive was reluctant to leave Fern on her own for long periods of time.

The couple were sitting at home one day, when Fern suddenly turned to Clive with an alarmed expression. 'I think my waters have broken,' she told him.

'That can't be possible,' he replied. The babies were not due for another four weeks, but Fern was adamant. As she was never one to mince her words, Clive realised that something must be up. Trusting his wife's judgment, he bundled her into the car and drove straight to the hospital. He barely had time to grab an overnight bag. Convinced the birth was still a fair way off, he and Fern had made little preparation.

Fern gave birth to two little boys on 14 December 1993. Because of complications resulting from her fibroid tumour, she had no option but to have a caesarean section. Clive did his best to allay her fears and remained by her side throughout the birth. After a little deliberation, they both settled on the names Harry and Jack. Sadly, the new parents had barely any time to spend with their boys. Both were rushed to the special care baby unit at High Wycombe Hospital. Harry had particular problems with his breathing. 'What's wrong?' cried Fern, as the nurses bundled up her twins. Although weary from the difficult birth, she could still summon up enough energy to protect her young. The nurses explained that there had been some complications during the birth. Fern was distraught, and, unable to control her emotions, she burst into tears. She had already been through a traumatic pregnancy and was not sure how much more she could take.

Watching her newborns in pain was unbearable. Even now, she vividly recalls the image of Harry lying in a cot. 'He was in a terrible state with tubes coming out of his mouth so that he couldn't even get his finger into his mouth to suck.' It was an horrific sight. Clive tried to comfort Fern. 'It's OK,' he promised. 'He'll make it though. He's a little fighter. He won't be beaten. Just look at him!'

Thankfully, Clive was right. Harry refused to give up. 'Even then he showed he was a fighter,' said Fern. 'He was getting red in the face trying to pull the tubes out.' And while Harry showed signs of improvement, Fern refused to leave his side. Instead, she kept a twenty-four-hour vigil, sensitive to every change of breathing or small movement. Clive tried desperately to convince Fern that she should rest, but his pleas fell on deaf ears. There was no way she was moving. Her attention was 100 per cent on Harry. She feared that if she turned her back for even one moment, something terrible might happen. Resting helplessly in the cot, Harry would look longingly up at her. 'He used to lie there and watch me as the tears rolled down my face,' she recalled, still choking at the memory.

Eventually, Harry was given the all clear and Fern had

permission to take her two boys home. She felt an overwhelming sense of relief. Clive had gone to great lengths to ensure his family's homecoming was as smooth as possible. He cleaned the house thoroughly and made sure that the fridge was well stocked with food. He and Fern had already kitted out the nursery in preparation for the birth. Pictures of animals adorned the walls, while a selection of stuffed toys filled every available space. While passing by a gift shop in town, Clive had noticed a display of helium balloons. Inspired, he went inside and purchased several to decorate the nursery and carefully arranged them round the bars of each cot.

Even though Fern took to motherhood like a duck to water, she did encounter a few early hiccups. She was, after all, exploring uncharted territory. Fortunately, Clive was on hand to give Fern some valuable advice. He already had three teenage children from a previous marriage and was a dab hand at parenting. 'That's probably the benefit of being an older father,' he told friends. 'Because you don't get wound up about changing nappies and so on.'

Fern gushed at length about how wonderful her husband was around the house. He was always willing to muck in and forever telling Fern to put her feet up. If ever the boys woke up in the night, the pair would take it in turns to care for them. Fern could not praise Clive enough. 'He's been brilliant, first of all in coping with me

when I wasn't very well towards the end of the pregnancy and then having him there during the caesarean – because I was a bit scared. Then Clive is genuinely into babies and wonderful at calming them down.'

Clive was not the only man to offer his support: Fern's father, Tony, also proved to be a pillar of strength. He was already a grandfather to Fern's elder sister Cherry's three children. Cherry was married to Brian Cant, the star of the children's television programme *Play Away*. Tony loved spending time with them and was overjoyed when Fern announced that she was starting a family of her own. On the day that Fern and the twins arrived home from hospital, Tony was waiting to greet her. He presented the two baby boys with authentic English teddy bears. Fern still had the bear 'Dada' had given her some thirty-six years previously, which, as a child, she had treasured dearly and it had accompanied her all over the world. Each night, she would hold it tightly and fall asleep thinking of her father. Having weathered a few storms over the years, he was now a little dog-eared with tufts of fur missing, but she still kept him as a memento of her childhood.

Fern loved watching Tony with her children; it brought back memories of her own childhood. Often, Tony would put the boys to sleep. Fern would creep into the nursery and eavesdrop on the bedtime stories that he liked to tell. It always brought a smile to her face. Many of the stories she could almost recall word for word. He

was still as great a wordsmith as she remembered. 'Dad is very inventive with children,' she told Clive. 'He has a wonderful imagination and is always inventing imaginary characters.'

Tony was not the only doting grandparent – Fern's mother, Ruth, also took every opportunity to visit the twins and was forever spoiling them with gifts. She lived only twenty minutes from Fern and Clive and was more than happy to offer to baby-sit. Fern was extremely close to her mother and frequently turned to her for both practical and emotional advice. 'She's the most important person in my life apart from Clive and the babies,' Fern insisted at the time.

Although both Fern and Clive were overjoyed with their new family, neither had plans to extend it any further. The combined problems of age and Fern's health suggested that it was sensible to put the brakes on. There was a part of her that longed to have a little girl. She envisioned a future spent discussing clothes, make-up and eventually men. But she reasoned it was for the best. 'I assumed I would have a boy and a girl, but funnily enough when the boys came out, there was a moment where I felt disappointment at not having a daughter.'

For the time being, Fern and Clive had enough on the hands. Bringing up two young babies would be hard work! In all honesty Fern didn't mind making cutbacks in her social calendar. As a breakfast television presenter, working unsociable hours, she had become accustomed

to staying in of an evening. Both she and Clive enjoyed relaxing in front of the television or listening to music. But that did not mean that they were loners! Quite the contrary, the couple were always entertaining guests. Friends would comment on how instantly welcome they felt when stepping through the door and were always eager to make return visits. 'We're basically very sedate people,' shrugged Fern. 'People come to our house a lot but we pretty much lived a quiet life before. We didn't go out very much.'

Although confident in her skills as a mother, Fern was under no illusion that it would be an easy task. Clive suggested that they employ someone to help out. Although Fern was reluctant to do so at first, after some persuasion she came round to the idea. On the recommendation of a friend, Fern employed a young lady called Jenny. She would help trouble-shoot for a couple of months, just while Fern settled in with the twins. After that, Fern could reassess the situation and consider some longer-term and more permanent assistance.

Thankfully, the bosses at *GMTV* were extremely understanding and offered Fern all the support she needed. She was a national treasure and worth far too much to the station. They would do everything in their power to keep her. Even during her absence, the studio had been inundated with cards and messages of goodwill. Fern was extremely touched and even shed a tear when presented with a pile of fan mail. Wiping away the tears, she joked that her sentimental turn was all down to hormones! She was overwhelmed by so much attention and could not understand what she had done to deserve it. Her father, Tony, however, was more easily convinced. 'Fern is wonderfully extrovert and the lovely thing about her is that she is exactly the same when you meet her in real life as she is on the screen,' he said in praise of his daughter. 'Her vivacity, sense of fun and enjoyment of life are her. She doesn't have to put it on.'

When Fern did eventually return to work, her hours were fortunately not quite so gruelling. Having worked the graveyard slot for breakfast television, anything else seemed like a breeze in comparison. 'With "Top Of The Morning" I don't have to get up until 5.30!' she exclaimed with relief. 'They send me a wonderful driver who comes and collects me at 6.30. I get into the back with my hair dripping wet and all the papers are there on the back seat. I get to work, do the programme and often I can be home by lunchtime. I've got a cushy number really. So fingers crossed, it might not be too much of a problem with the twins.'

But if her workload ever became too much, Fern was determined to put her family first. Even in the light of her success, she had never confused her priorities. She was a mother, wife and daughter first; a television presenter second. 'I do love working and I have really enjoyed everything I have done, but if it all stopped now because of the babies, I would still be a happy woman,' she smiled.

The past few months had been a difficult ride, but unfortunately Fern was not out of the woods just yet. Sadly, there were more troubles in store. For the first few weeks after Harry and Jack's birth, she was too busy with the twins to even think about herself. She was lucky if she had more than a straight four hours' sleep a night! Breastfeeding the twins left her physically drained and she could not leave them unattended for even a minute. Every night she would collapse into bed, her feet throbbing. Acknowledging his cue, Clive would bring his wife a cup of tea and treat her to a soothing foot massage. It was absolute bliss.

As it turned out, however, Fern had more than just the physical strain to deal with. The emotional pressure was starting to mount. One day, while doing the laundry, she suddenly felt a rush of despair. The skies darkened and the world around her caved in. She felt dizzy and uneasy on her feet. Grabbing the side of the washing machine, she tried to balance herself. She could sense the bitter taste of panic in the back of her throat. Breathing deeply, she tried to focus by counting each breath. Within a few minutes the panic subsided, but it was quickly replaced by an overwhelming sense of pointlessness. The house she had once found so welcoming took on new cruel and imposing characteristics. The walls seemed to be closing in on her. She could almost feel the bricks and mortar crushing her chest. For the first time in her life, Fern felt utterly alone.

'I felt very isolated and quite dark, very quickly,' she said, recalling that difficult period. Once she had managed to compose herself, Fern picked up the phone to call Clive and tell him what had happened. Her fingers were trembling as she dialled the numbers. But just as she went to tap in the last digit, she hung up. How on earth could she put into words exactly what had just happened?

The panic attacks continued. They would always set in at the most inopportune moments. Once they started, Fern could do nothing. She wished there was a way she could switch off her emotions and block out the pain, but there was never any escape. Even Clive found it difficult to understand her constant mood swings. Fern understood it was not his fault. After all, how on earth could he understand what was going on in her head? It was Jack and Harry that she worried about the most. She desperately hoped that they would never sense her unhappiness. The depressive mood swings would range from mild to severe, but at their worst they were unbearable.

'I can remember one evening when the boys were bathed and everything was sorted and I was trying to be jolly, but inside I was thinking, "I'll just nip outside and kill myself,"' said Fern. 'Not because I wanted to, but because I just wanted it to stop.' It was not the only occasion on which Fern had suicidal thoughts: 'I also remember getting overwhelming urges to get in the car and drive into a brick wall. I think this kind of depression is like mental tinnitus. You just want to turn it off or turn it down.'

Coping with twins was proving to be more of a struggle than Fern had initially anticipated. Burdened with double the workload of a new mother, she found herself under an extreme amount of pressure. With no prior experience of bringing up children, she spent most of the time feeling her way in the dark. During the night she would wake up in a sweat, panicking that she was not ready to cope with so much responsibility. Had she changed their nappies properly? Were they eating the right food? Could she give them enough love and attention? These were all fears that raced through her mind. She would lie awake for several minutes before getting up to check on the boys. 'I think it was a big shock to the system to have two at once,' she reasoned with hindsight.

Soon after the birth, Fern also broke her right wrist. Being right-handed, this caused a number of problems. Her mother's help, Jenny, had to do most of the work. 'I couldn't bathe the boys, feed them, or even lift them, and I was so frustrated. I felt like a failure because I could not even do the simplest things,' she complained. Fed up with sitting on the sidelines, she attempted to change the boys' nappies. However, it was an impossible task. Angry with herself, Fern broke down in tears.

Fern convinced herself that a return to work would help her snap out of the depression. At least she would be surrounded by people and too distracted to wallow in self-pity. Sadly, the television studio afforded little sanctuary. Even though a million-odd viewers tuned in to watch Fern every day, she had never felt more alone. All the while, however, she tried to put on a brave face. Fern Britton depressed? How ridiculous! She was the happy, chirpy television presenter who brought sunshine to every rainy day. There was no way she could tell anyone the truth. Under no circumstances could she let people down.

So she smiled for the cameras and struggled to keep up appearances. All the while she was tearing up inside. Whenever she did feel a bout of depression coming on, Fern would make her excuses and dash to the toilets, or seek refuge in her dressing room. 'I remember going into the dressing room smiling and laughing,' she recalled. 'But once inside, I'd stand up so the tears could just fall on the floor – and I'd do it silently in case anyone would hear. Then I'd mop myself up and go back into the studio.' These bouts of crying were not uncommon. Fern could rarely predict when another would strike. She had lost complete control of her emotions and had no idea what was happening to her body: 'In the car going home, I'd just look out of the window with tears running down my face.'

Fern soldiered on alone for as long as possible. After a while, the low moments became almost familiar. When her daily panic attacks set in, she embraced them with a perverse sense of comfort. Tired of fighting the pain, she resigned herself to feeling that way for the rest of life. But eventually, something had to give. Unable to resist it any longer, Fern finally broke down. 'The day it all came to head was when it had taken me three days to paint my toenails,' recalled Fern. 'I'd applied a coat a day and my hands were full with two little boys who were just being normal and happy, but I couldn't cope. They were seven months old at the time. I was crumpled on the bed, and I think I was crying – I was always crying then.'

At the time, Fern's mother, Ruth, was downstairs in the kitchen preparing dinner for the twins. She was frantically searching for a tin opener. She had been through every cupboard and opened every drawer, but could not find one anywhere. 'Fern,' she called, 'where have you hidden the tin opener?' But there was no response. She went to the foot of the stairs and shouted a little louder. Still nothing. As she started to climb the stairs she could hear a faint sobbing in the distance. Pushing open the bedroom door gently, she walked in to find her daughter rolled up in a ball on the bed. Globules of nail varnish were dripping from an upturned pot on the bedside table. 'What's the matter?' she asked, concern rising in her voice. Kneeling down beside Fern, she lifted her head and looked her directly in the eyes. 'I'm going to ring the doctor,' she said firmly. 'Because you're not well.'

The doctor came out and examined Fern. He concluded she was suffering from postnatal depression. But this was more than just the 'baby blues' – Fern needed medical help. The doctor sat down with Fern and explained the

45

syndrome. It was not uncommon. One in eight new mothers developed postnatal depression within a few days or weeks of the birth, with either a slow or sudden onset. Fern was displaying all the classic symptoms: low self-esteem, lack of confidence, inadequacy, disturbed sleep and tearfulness. He went on to inform her that support from friends and family was crucial to the patient's recovery. He suggested it might also be useful to speak with a counsellor or one of the many support networks in the area. As Fern's condition was quite severe, he decided to prescribe her anti-depressants. However, he reassured her that postnatal depression was a temporary disorder that would heal with time.

Fern was placed on a course of the controversial drug Prozac. There had been a backlash against the drug sparked by David Healy's book *Let Them Eat Prozac*. Critics claimed that the drug made people suicidal and caused several other serious side effects. Subsequently, the American pharmaceutical manufacturers Eli Lilly and Company were presented with lawsuits amounting to millions of dollars. But these did little to affect the popularity of the drug. In Fern's case, Prozac proved to be helpful. Over time, her moods lifted and it gave her just the boost she needed to get back on track with her life. She would later go on to describe it as a 'wonderful drug'.

With hindsight, Fern realised her bouts of depression had started during childhood. At the time she had never recognised them as such: Unable to identify the black cloud that swathed her emotions, she had simply put it down to a bad day. As a girl she did not realise that depression was a medical condition. Given her past history, she was extremely susceptible to continued attacks in adult life. Any slight emotional upheaval was likely to cause problems. But once she understood exactly what was going on with her body, Fern felt an incredible sense of relief. 'I've suffered from moments of depression since I was a child but I didn't know what they were. But once you've faced up to the fact that it is an illness and somebody has diagnosed it as such, it is such a relief.'

Fern recalls that her family was incredibly supportive throughout this difficult time. Many of them were shocked to discover that she had been feeling so unhappy. On the outside she appeared so calm and light-hearted. Perhaps Fern was a better actress than she had once imagined! All those years spent working in the theatre had obviously effected her. 'It's amazing how you can smile when inside you're shrivelling. You wake up feeling really tired and think, "I can't get out of bed," but you push yourself to get up and make it through the day.'

Even today, Fern shudders at the memory of that dark period. She felt permanently exhausted and barely had enough strength to cope with even the simplest of tasks. Sometimes, making a simple cup of tea seemed an insurmountable task and it was during these low moments that Clive really rose to the occasion and supported his wife. Giving her a hug, he promised that things would get better.

It was tough, but gradually life started to feel brighter. Slowly Fern was beginning to regain control of her life and her emotions. She cites a turning point as the moment when she felt strong enough to accept her responsibilities as a mother: 'I do remember having one hard day with the twins, crying and wanting to call my mum, and then realising that she was out at lunch and feeling so low and like I could not cope. And then I realised, no, I'm the mum now, the buck has to stop with me.'

It was a major breakthrough. For the first time, Fern felt able to survive the day completely alone. By focusing her attention on Jack and Harry, she pulled herself out of a rut.

Although much of Fern's depression was down to a chemical imbalance, she now believes there were several other contributory factors. During her pregnancy, Fern had suffered from extreme fatigue. Her energy levels were completely zapped. On her feet all day, she barely had time to eat properly. Speaking to her doctor months later, she realised that she had been missing out on nutrients vital to a healthy pregnancy. Even once the twins were born, Fern did little to improve her diet. She would often snack on scraps and leftovers rather than cook a proper meal. Whenever possible, Clive would make sure she had a healthy dinner, but during the day he was not always around to make sure Fern was looking after herself properly. 'I think that as a mum you are at the bottom of the pecking order and you don't take care of yourself,' she commented.

'I suffered from moments of bone-crushing tiredness all the time. I could hardly put one foot in front of the other,' Fern recalled. 'It was that really debilitating exhaustion that makes you feel so terrible. It hit me like a ton of bricks, but once I started taking medication, it helped.'

After months of stress and turmoil, Fern could finally enjoy being a mother. It had been a bumpy ride, but at last the road seemed to be levelling and she was heading for a clear patch. Life was slowly returning to normal, but it would not happen overnight.

Chapter 3

Ready Steady Cook

In order to concentrate on bringing up Jack and Harry, Fern decided to take a break in her career. Juggling the responsibilities of motherhood with the demands of a television studio only seemed to exacerbate her depression. For years, Fern had tried to do the impossible, but it was time to accept that she was only human. She had to let go. She had always told herself that family would come first, and friends and family agreed that a break from work would do Fern the world of good.

At first Fern found it hard to adjust to her new role. For several weeks, she would wake up at 5.30 am bright-eyed, expecting her car to be waiting outside. On one occasion she even went to get in the shower, before realising that she no longer needed to be up at the crack of dawn. Once

Fern had learned to deal with her postnatal depression, she actually began to enjoy parenting. By all accounts, she was a fantastic mother.

After a while, she became used to the routine of being a housewife. Working in television seemed a lifetime away. The vivacious, confident and outgoing Fern Britton who had captured the hearts of a viewing public seemed to be a completely different woman. Sometimes Fern would switch on the television and feel a sense of longing. She did miss her colleagues. But equally, the idea of returning to television was a daunting prospect. Seven months of caring for the twins had left her happy but drained. Her long-running battle with her weight gain had also taken a turn for the worst.

Before her pregnancy, Fern had trimmed herself down to a healthy size fourteen. It had been hard work, but she was extremely proud of her efforts. Everyone had commented on how great she looked. But like any new mother, Fern's body had taken a battering during her pregnancy. The extra pounds she had gained seemed impossible to shift. While that extra jam doughnut might have seemed justifiable at the time, she was now paying the price. The old excuse of eating for two (or three in Fern's case) had done her no great favours. 'Being pregnant with the twins, I put on two stone,' she winced, before adding, 'which is nothing for twins.'

Ironically, Fern had lost her excess weight instantly after giving birth. Much of that was probably due to the stress and worry. Unfortunately, the weight quickly piled back on: 'When they were about four or five months old, bang! Two stone went on like that. And I haven't got rid of it!' Fern felt extremely low. At first her jeans felt a little tight, then a week later, she found herself having trouble fastening the top button. 'I must have shrunk them in the wash!' she thought to herself. But gradually it became apparent that the problem was her waistline rather than her washing machine.

She blamed much of her weight gain on comfort eating. 'I think I was knackered. And because I was knackered and breastfeeding, and working and, blah, blah, blah, I fell into bags of doughnuts at every moment of the day,' she sighed. 'I think it's the fat content, and the sugar and the jam and the bread. So I think that's what did it really.'

Whatever the cause, Fern felt extremely unhappy with her body. Her weight gain made her even more reluctant to return to television. The camera famously piles on pounds and she dreaded how large she might appear. More importantly, she feared television bosses would be reluctant to offer her contracts. At her lowest ebb, Fern was convinced her career had reached a premature end. She resigned herself to being a mother and housewife. All things considered, it was not actually a bad option. 'I had a loss of confidence,' she said. 'I didn't think anyone would offer me work again. That was fine. I was a happy bunny at home. I wanted to spend as much time with the children as I could.'

Then one day, completely out of the blue, Fern received a call from her agent. At the time, she was clearing away breakfast debris and subsequently a little distracted – the boys had a habit of chucking as much food on the floor as they did in their mouth! After exchanging pleasantries for a few minutes, her agent turned to the matter in hand: 'Listen Fern, what are your thoughts about returning to work?'

'Um… I haven't really thought about it too much,' she replied, using a dishcloth to mop up a rather disgusting looking globule of mashed banana.

'It's just that a show has come up and we think you'd be perfect,' the agent continued.

'Hmm,' mumbled Fern, spying another lump of mush dripping from the fridge door. Sometimes she did wonder how something so small could make so much mess.

'It's a new cookery show and we'd like you to audition for presenter,' her agent continued.

Suddenly Fern clicked back into reality and she registered exactly what her agent was proposing. 'I don't know,' said Fern reluctantly. 'I think perhaps you've asked the wrong person.'

Her agent proceeded to give her more details. The show would be called *Ready Steady Cook* and would air on daytime television. The premise was simple: two members of the public would present a couple of celebrity chefs with a bag of ingredients, set to a budget of £5. Split into two teams, the chefs would then have twenty minutes to prepare a selection of dishes from the ingredients supplied, with the help of the contestants and the programme host. The ultimate winner would receive a cash prize of £100 for a charity of their choice.

The idea that Fern should present a cookery programme was practically laughable. She had never been particularly creative in the kitchen. Beans on toast or scrambled eggs were about as ambitious as she got. Clive often joked that she was the queen of ready-made meals. She was not about to humiliate herself in front of millions by demonstrating her lack of culinary skills. 'I hated cooking and wasn't very good at it,' Fern admitted. As a child, home economics had been her worst subject. Her teacher even cruelly told Fern she would never amount to anything in the kitchen.

Fern cast her mind back. Every week, she dreaded attending the lesson. She was certain that the teacher had a vendetta against her because she would constantly criticise Fern for being messy and incompetent, which made Fern feel even worse. Everyone in the class had been instructed to follow a recipe for fisherman's pie. Dutifully, Fern had collected together all the correct ingredients. Determined to prove her teacher wrong, she pain-stakingly measured out each of the ingredients. But as she followed the guidelines on her recipe card, she could feel her teacher's glare burning into her back like a laser beam. Suffering a loss of confidence, she dropped her utensils on the floor. The loud crash sound brought everyone in the class to a halt. The teacher smirked. This was exactly the mistake she had been waiting for. Taking great pleasure in making a mockery of Fern, she dragged the frightened little girl to the front of the class.

'She was a hateful woman!' spat Fern, in an uncharacteristic display of rage. 'She loathed and humiliated me.' As a punishment for her clumsiness, the teacher forced Fern to finish her recipe in full public view. 'She made me mash 5lb of potatoes with a two-pronged fork in front of the whole class. And, according to her, I couldn't even do that right!'

The whole incident left a very bitter taste in Fern's mouth and ever since that moment she had despised cooking, convinced that she had the culinary skills of a ten-year-old.

But her agent was not going to take 'no' for an answer. He had always believed in Fern and was not about to watch her talent go to waste just because she was suffering a loss of self-confidence. The show would be an ideal re-introduction into the world of television. It was exactly the kick-start she needed to fire up her career. 'It will do you good!' he insisted. 'At least do it for your fans. People are dying to see you again.'

But Fern was adamant that she had made up her mind. 'Please,' her agent begged. 'At least attend the audition and see how you feel. It won't cost you anything to have a go. If nothing else, please do it for me.' She did not want to upset her agent, who had become a good friend over

An early shot of Fern Britton from when she was just starting out in her broadcasting career.

The changing style but ever-smiling face of Fern Britton.

Bottom right: A rare picture of Fern with first husband Clive Jones.

© REX Features

Top: Fern with fellow breakfast TV presenters Audrey Eyton and Esther Rantzen, 1983.

Bottom left: Fern arriving at an award ceremony with youngest daughter Winnie, 2002.

Bottom right: Fern's father, actor Tony Britton.

Fern has made dozens of famous friends during her career.

Top left: Nick Owen co-presented the documentary *Airport 90* with Fern in 1990.

Top right: While on GMTV, Fern and Lorraine Kelly became close friends as they supported each other through their pregnancies.

Bottom left: Chefs Anthony Worrall Thompson and Brian Turner are just two of the stars from *Ready Steady Cook* who Fern counts among her friends.

Bottom right: Fern stood by *This Morning* co-host John Leslie when he was accused of rape.

Top: Determined to get in shape before her first bike race, Fern enlisted the help of fitness experts to help her prepare for a charity ride.

Bottom: At the starting line in Egypt. Fern has used her public profile to raise thousands of pounds for good causes, as well as supporting a host of organisations including Women's Aid, Women for Women, the ante- and postnatal illness support charity PNI-UK and Epilepsy Action.

Top and bottom left: A Formula 1 fan and self-confessed speed junkie, Fern jumped at the chance to try and 'beat the boys' on Ant and Dec's *Saturday Night Takeaway*.

Bottom right: Fern was excited at the thought of becoming a motorcycle courier for the BBC programme *Danger, Celebrity at Work* in 2001.

BUMPER ISSUE!

Woman's Realm

December 21/28 1999 £1·20

PARTY MAKEOVERS

'We want a new look for Christmas'

£8,000 IN FREE GIFTS!

MAEVE BINCHY
Heart-warming short story

PLUS • Diana Ross
• George Clooney
• Michael Douglas

TIME TO CELEBRATE!
6 pages of the most beautiful dresses ever

FERN
I'm in love with a wonderful guy

4-PAGE TAROT SPECIAL
Your personal reading reveals the year ahead

MERRY CHRISTMAS!

In a bid to deal with her approaching 40s and show she is proud of her curves, Fern posed for a series of revealing photos in *Family Circle* magazine. Many of her admirers are loud and proud about their love for Fern's fuller figure – including actor Dominic Monaghan (*bottom right*)!

Bottom Left: Fern demonstrating her specs appeal with Kate Thornton, Howard Brown and Patsy Kensit at the Spectacle Wearer of the Year Commission, 2002.

'I would rather be big and happy than on a diet and miserable.'

A triumphant Fern at the National Television Awards with her gong for most popular daytime TV programme.

the past few years and who, as it turned out, was also terminally ill. So Fern reluctantly agreed and, looking back, was glad that she had done so, not least because it had delighted her agent.

In the days leading up to the audition, Fern felt extremely nervous. It had been so long since she had stood in front of a camera. She wondered if she had forgotten what to do. Fortunately, she laid out an outfit the night before. Looking in the mirror, she convinced herself to just go for it. She had come this far and there was no turning back. When she arrived at the studios, she was ushered into a green room and offered tea and coffee. Two more women joined her. Fern made polite conversation and discovered that they were also auditioning for the position. Her heart sank. Any confidence she had managed to summon up instantly dissipated. She felt completely crushed. She did not stand a chance in hell.

'There were three women up for the presenter's job,' she recalled. 'The other two were very young and very famous. And there was me – the old bat – so I really didn't think I stood much of a chance.'

Convinced that she was an outside bet, Fern relaxed a little. She had nothing to lose so she thought she might as well go out there and enjoy the audition. But then something unexpected happened.

'I wasn't worried about it until I did the audition and realised I was enjoying myself,' she explained.

Suddenly, Fern was back in the running. She wanted this job and was not prepared to give up without a fight. 'I remember thinking, "I want this job more than anything I've wanted in years." But I really thought they'd give it to one of the pretty young chicks.'

Thankfully, they did not. The producers were extremely impressed by Fern's mild manner and found her talents ideally suited to the show. Within minutes she had the crew in stitches with her friendly banter. She fired a round of ridiculous questions at the chefs and was not afraid to muck in and get her hands dirty. Everyone agreed that Fern should take on the role. There was no competition.

When her agent called with the good news, Fern was over the moon. For the first time in months, she felt genuinely excited about returning to work. But she was still anxious about leaving her children at home. She aired her concerns with the production team and thankfully they were extremely sympathetic to Fern's situation. The schedule was flexible and the bosses were prepared to work around Fern. 'The show fitted really well into my life,' said Fern. 'It was only three days a week every fortnight because we recorded three shows back to back. That meant I could spend lots of time with the kids.'

Fern was extremely flattered. The fact that she had managed to land such a plum job was proof indeed that age and body shape could never detract from core talent. It was also proof that motherhood did not necessarily spell the end to a successful career. Fern felt proud to be an inspiration to millions of working mothers in Britain. The first show aired in 1994. Although everyone involved had great faith in the project, no one could have predicted just how successful it would be. It garnered a cult following among housewives and students and some people even tuned in just to watch Fern.

In marked contrast to her darker days of depression, Fern would wake up looking forward to the day ahead. She had a new zest for life and for the first time in months she was back to her old self. Not every battle, however, had been won. Fern continued to struggle with her fluctuating waistline. Working on a cookery show was hardly conducive to dieting! Critics suggested that Fern should steer clear of all the tempting dishes on offer. At one point it was even rumoured that she had ballooned to a size eighteen! Fern was quick to set the record straight: 'But it wouldn't matter if I was a size eighteen. It's how you feel that matters, not what you look like.'

She also pointed out that her weight gain was not an occupational hazard associated with working on *Ready Steady Cook*. She blamed most of the extra pounds she had put on on post-pregnancy doughnut binges. 'I love everything sweet!' she complained. 'My weakness is chocolate and cakes. I'd be perfectly happy to skip a main meal and go straight to the pud.'

On a number of occasions she had tried to forego desserts, but always ended up salivating over everyone else's dinner. She recalled what her father, Tony, had told her years previously: food was a pleasure, not something to feel imprisoned by. 'Isn't food supposed to be a pleasure?' she asked again. 'Real women aren't a perfect size ten.'

If anything, working on a cookery programme was actually helping Fern to slim. 'These days I'm not too worried about shape and size. I am just not bothered about food any more, I'm not hungry.' Fern linked her loss of appetite directly to the show. Contrary to popular belief, being around food all day was actually a turn off. 'I think it's a lot to do with *Ready Steady*,' she explained. 'It's like working in a sweet shop, I see food all the time, smell it, and I'm not interested.'

'People think I eat food on the show – I don't. I'm too busy changing for the next show. We do three a day. And they think that I live in a whirl of invitations to restaurants. I don't have that.'

Although some people might like to believe otherwise, Fern did not lead a glamorous lifestyle. While other celebrities were attending premieres and charity galas, Fern was at home changing nappies and washing baby-gros. And though people continued to make comments about her weight, she managed to ignore most of them. 'I can get beyond the scrutiny on TV,' she shrugged. 'Because the person who does *Ready Steady Cook* I can see is somebody else. It's another woman I know, and it's all on her, poor old thing. And me? It doesn't touch me.'

For every critic, Fern had an army of admirers. Praised

for her rounded and voluptuous figure, she became something of an alternative sex symbol. One men's magazine even referred to her as a 'culinary Moll Flanders' and a 'mumsy vixen'. Fern was both amused and flattered by such comments. Gradually, she was learning to love her new bumps and lumps. Men would constantly stop her in the street to pay compliments. One of the best chat-up lines came from an admirer in New York. At the time, Fern was celebrating New Year in the Big Apple. Minding her own business, she was strolling through downtown Manhattan when she heard a guy wolf whistle behind her. 'This great big black man walked past and said… "Hey lady, you are BUILT!"' she laughed.

For once, Fern started to take pride in her curves. She could never carry off the clothes that stick-thin models such as Kate Moss might wear, but that did not mean to say that she could not look sexy. 'I still feel like a TV chick,' she told reporters at the time. 'I believe that when *Ready Steady Cook* was first thought of, the powers that be wanted someone younger and "chickier". But the old trout won through. However, once you believe you're an old boot, you're lost. Always believe you're gorgeous.'

Although Fern had her workload largely in hand, increasing demands were made on her time as *Ready Steady Cook* grew in popularity. Recording the show was tiring, but Fern was enjoying the adrenalin rush. Then, out of the blue, the working mother discovered that she was pregnant again. Given the difficulties she had endured while expecting the twins, friends and family were shocked at the revelation. To their knowledge, Fern and Clive had little intention of expanding the family. With Fern's career firmly back on track, the timing also seemed inappropriate. Not everyone, however, was taken by surprise. Even before doctors could confirm that she was pregnant, Fern received confirmation from a psychic. Open to new-age schools of thought, she took the prediction extremely seriously. Even her unborn baby's name was communicated to Fern psychically.

It was a bright, sunny morning and Fern had decided to take the twins out for a walk. They had been bounding around the house all morning like caged animals and she decided a breath of fresh air would do them some good. 'Come on!' she said, gathering together a collection of coats and shoes. 'Let's go for a walk in the sunshine.' Jack was in a particularly obstinate mood and refused to stand still for one minute. Leaving the house was never an easy task and always required some serious preparation. 'Jack! Be good for Mummy,' she pleaded. Eventually he calmed down and agreed to cooperate.

As the weather was so fine, Fern decided to take a drive into the countryside. She parked the car and decided to take a stroll along a public footpath. Looking up at the sky, she felt a rush of energy. Shards of sunlight pierced the canopy of trees overhead and danced gracefully on the footpath. Aside from the rustling of leaves underfoot, not a sound could be heard. Taking in a deep breath, Fern felt completely at peace. A small village church lay ahead and tempted by a mound of bluebells nodding gently in the breeze, she decided to take a detour. A narrow and slightly overgrown path led through a series of weathered gravestones. It set Fern of on a train of thought. She wondered what sort of lives these people had led. One stone in particular caught her eye. A small bouquet of fresh flowers had been arranged in a vase. She read the inscription: 'To Grace'. 'Such a beautiful and elegant name,' she thought to herself.

The memory of that gravestone remained with Fern for some time. Something about that moment had seemed so poignant – maybe it was the air, the light, or even the smell. She could not put her finger on it. It was not a memory as such, but a certain 'sense' or 'feeling'. When Fern finally gave birth to her daughter, that same thought returned. She knew then that it must be a sign and she chose to name her newborn daughter Grace Alice Bluebell. 'I was given Grace's name psychically,' explained Fern. 'It was on a gravestone in a country churchyard where I was taking the twins for a walk. And she arrived at bluebell time.'

Unfortunately, Fern's actual pregnancy was not quite such a beautiful story. Once again, she had fibroid trouble. In most instances these 'horrible, lumpy tumours' occur inside the womb, but Fern's case was quite unusual. 'Mine was on the outside,' she explained. In the months leading up to Grace's birth, the growth caused her considerable pain. Inevitably, Fern again had to opt for a caesarian birth. It was not ideal, but she accepted that it was necessary. Having been through it once, she was able to handle it a second time around. Once Grace was born, Fern paid a visit to her gynaecologist to seek advice on her fibroid. 'Oh, that's a leave-well-alone job,' she was told.

Fern was just relieved to have survived the birth with relatively few complications. But her problems were not over. For a second time, Fern battled with postnatal weight gain. By now she was almost resigned to a few extra pounds. She had been down this road before. When it came to doughnuts and sweet foods, resistance was futile. There was no point in eating half an éclair, because ten minutes later she would be back to finish the whole lot. Pregnancy, and the difficulties her particular case entailed, left Fern feeling exhausted. She needed all those extra calories just to make it through the day. 'When I was expecting Grace I went up to thirteen stone eight pounds just before she was born,' admitted Fern.

Whereas in the past Fern might have fretted over her weight gain, now she simply accepted it as a given. Besides, after caring for a newborn for several weeks, any extra baggage would soon disappear – and Fern's prediction was 100 per cent spot on. Once back at home, the weight flew off. Caring for three young children certainly beat any gym work-out! 'That's the wonderful thing about having a baby,' she beamed. 'A week later you've lost two stone.' At 5 feet 7 inches tall, Fern hovered around a healthy size twelve.

But there were several logistical problems! Fern's chest had ballooned in the preceding weeks. 'Bosoms can get in the way,' she sighed, looking back. 'When I was feeding the babies, I was about a 44H. Enormous. Like rockets. And very uncomfortable in bed. I had to sleep in a bra!' she continued with amazement. 'I couldn't not have a bra on. To take it off was quite something.' Thankfully, the pain did not last for too long. 'They shrink back!' she smiled. Within a matter of months, Fern was down to a 38 or 36DD. But there was a point when she seriously considered a breast reduction.

'I did go through a stage when I stopped breastfeeding Gracie, when I thought, "I'm going to have to get something done. I'm going to have to get them hoiked up. Reduced and hoiked up surgically,"' she confessed.

Fern had reached breaking point after a particularly strenuous day. She had been on her feet all day and the strain on her back was unbearable, and she was also sick and tired of the restrictions a large chest imposed. Hardly any tops fitted her properly and running up and down the stairs was absolute agony. She could not imagine why some women would pay to have breasts this big! Quite the contrary: she dreamed they might actually shrink overnight.

As it turned out, Fern was spared the trauma of going under the surgeon's knife. Being honest with herself, surgery was never really an option. 'I thought, "Ooh, no, I just don't think I really could,"' she admitted. To her relief, a close friend came up with a much better idea. The luxury lingerie store Rigby and Peller, based in Knightsbridge in London, sold a special range of comfortable support bras in larger sizes. 'I went to Rigby and Peller, bought a couple of good bras and that's much better. Only fifty quid and no pain.'

On her visit, Fern fell in love with the store. She spent a good hour sifting through delicate silky French knickers and embroidered bras. She was amazed to find underwear in her size that actually looked attractive! 'Rigby and Peller are a fantastic underwear shop!' she told friends. 'No matter what size, what shape, they've got everything – pretty ones, sports bras, matching knickers, all colours.'

As soon as Fern arrived home, she could not wait to admire her new purchases. 'Sexy, but large!' she concluded, holding a lace-trimmed pair of panties up to the light. More people than Fern imagined managed to catch a glimpse of her new lingerie. 'Seeing them hanging on the line, somebody said to me, "A couple of seagulls could nest in there!"' she joked. It was not quite the response she had hoped for!

Although Fern was overjoyed by a new addition to her family, any happy thoughts were overshadowed by the fear that her debilitating postnatal depression might rear its ugly head once again. Sadly, it did. Even though Fern recognised the symptoms, it did not make them any easier to deal with. Simple tasks became major undertakings and she found it difficult to summon up enough energy even to get out of bed in the morning. She felt just like she had done three years previously after giving birth to the twins. Only this time round, she knew what to do about it. Without hesitation, she sought help from her doctor. While there was no miracle cure for depression, she could at least seek a helping hand.

With three children to look after, Fern was rushed off her feet at the best of times. As a mother she was on duty twenty-four hours a day. Then, of course, she had her career to consider. Though determined that her family would always come first, Fern was not about to give up *Ready Steady Cook*. The production team was extremely understanding and ready to offer Fern whatever help she required, but the cracks soon started to show. Inevitably, something had to give and, sadly, it turned out to be Fern's marriage.

Even today, Fern refuses to discuss the specific reasons behind the failure of her marriage. The whole ordeal was painful enough. The last thing she wanted was a public audience. She also had too much respect for Clive and her children. All she has said on the matter is: 'The break-up of my marriage is very private. No one else is involved.' Ultimately, she blamed the 'pressure of work'.

But the split was reportedly less than amicable and Fern plunged into a further depression. While on the outside she tried to keep up appearances, inside she was falling apart. She feared the impact the split would have on her children. They were the innocent bystanders who would ultimately suffer and Fern knew that from her own childhood experience. 'Getting divorced is not easy and the ripple effect goes through your whole family. Plus I was working hard and my daughter Gracie was only a year old.'

But far from being an unwelcome pressure, *Ready Steady Cook* provided Fern with some welcome relief. In the studio she could focus completely on the job in hand and forget about her own life for a few hours. Nobody had a clue. As far as they were concerned, Fern was simply a little over-tired which was natural for a mother of three. But once the camera lights had dimmed and she was on her way home, the nagging emotional pain would set in. A simple memory would send her off on a train of thought. She was extremely tense and even the slightest problem seemed to spell the end of the world. Sitting in the back seat of her chauffer-driven car, she would stare out of the window looking for some sort of light distraction. Sadly, it never came. Instead, she had time to reflect on the broken home to which she was returning. Without warning, tears would stream down her face. Using a tissue, she tried to stem their flow, but it was a useless exercise. After a few attempts, she simply let them roll to the floor. '*Ready Steady Cook* was partly my salvation because I could go to work and forget about everything else. But I would be in floods of tears all the way home in the car.'

After a difficult period, the estranged couple agreed that Fern should look after the children. Clive would, however, be completely involved in their lives. Accepting the end of her marriage filled Fern with extreme sadness. It was a situation that she had never quite imagined. Bringing up a family and holding down a career had never been easy – now it was about to get even harder. But Fern was determined. She had been at rock bottom before and always managed to climb back up to the top. From now on, she would channel all her energies into bringing up her children and if that meant being single for the rest of her life, then so be it.

Chapter 4

Big and Proud

Although divorce ran in Fern's family, nothing could prepare her for the pain of a break-up. Her levels of motivation slumped to an all-time low and the enjoyment slowly faded from every aspect of her life. Had she been alone, she would probably have gone under, but with her kids in mind, she managed to keep her head above water. Once up and dressed, she had little time to worry about her own problems. The demands of bringing up a family alone were extremely high.

However, being a single parent did give Fern some time to reflect on her mother's situation. Coping with two young kids cannot have been easy. She had always sympathised with her mother, but now she fully understood and she was overwhelmed with admiration for Ruth. The two began to speak more regularly on the phone. If ever Fern needed a shoulder to cry on, she would turn to her mother. If one benefit came out of this whole sorry mess, it was that mother and daughter forged a stronger bond. 'Once I became a single parent myself, I suppose my mother was a bit of a role model for me,' she smiles. 'In fact, I came from a long line of single mothers – my mother, grandmother and great-grandmother were all single parents, mostly because of divorce.'

Knowing that her mother had survived alone and successfully managed to bring up two children gave Fern much-needed strength. Looking back at her own childhood, she had few complaints. Even though there had been bumpy moments, the good times far outweighed the bad and she was determined to give her children the same opportunities. 'It wasn't quite so frightening for me to be on my own,' admits Fern. 'I had seen how my mother coped brilliantly with bringing us up.'

After the split, Clive had agreed to move out of their £500,000, Tudor-style family home in Buckinghamshire. In the first few weeks after his departure, Fern sensed an eerie emptiness in the house. Memories of her marriage permeated every wall, every furnishing and every little knick-knack. Picking up various ornaments, she recalled in detail exactly when they had been purchased and she remembered how Clive had gone to so much trouble to decorate the nursery in preparation for her return from hospital with the twins. She smiled. It was a beautiful memory, now tinged with sadness.

But life went on. With three kids running riot, there was never a dull moment. Like any single woman, Fern had her up and her down days. Work was generally going well and being around adults during the day kept her sane. There had been adjustments to her lifestyle, but thus far Fern had managed to juggle being a single mother with holding down a successful career. 'Life is good,' she reflected in one of her more positive moments. 'I've had an incredibly exciting year at work and my children are healthy and happy.'

In spite of everything, Fern considered herself to be extremely fortunate. Unlike a lot of people, she looked forward to going in to work everyday. It was never a chore. The cast and crew were always in fits of giggles about some ridiculous situation or another, the hours would rush by and, before she knew it, Fern would be in the car on her way home. Occasionally, she felt a twinge of guilt. Was it wrong to feel this happy while her children were waiting for her at home? Was it responsible for a mother to go out every day and leave her kids with a child minder? It was a difficult decision to make. 'There's always that moment when you're about to leave for work when a little voice says, "Mummy, why do you have to go? I wanted to read you my Batman story."'

At times like that, Fern would crumble. 'Now my children are the most important thing in my life.

Naturally I feel guilty about working. I need to make time to be Mummy because, if I didn't, I'd go crackers.' Equally, however, Fern needed to make time for herself. If she did not get out now and then, she would be of no use to anyone. 'There are days when I think if I stay in the house for another minute I'll go mad. To be honest, there are those times when you're glad to be at work without people going "Mummy, Mummy" all the time. Motherhood can be terrifically tedious, which no one tells you and you're not allowed to admit.'

Ruth agreed with her daughter: under no circumstances should she feel guilty for pursuing a life of her own. No one in their right mind could accuse Fern of putting her own interests before those of her children.

With some reassurance from Ruth, Fern felt confident that she was doing the right thing. 'It's really all right, because I do spend a lot of time with them,' she insisted. 'I'm always there when they get up and I'm nearly always there when they go to bed and although I've been incredibly busy this year, I've still been able to spend lots of time with them. Gracie is ten months old and Jack and Harry are three, so they are lots of fun to be around.'

By now, the twins had developed their own very distinctive personalities and Fern loved watching them grow into little boys. It seemed like only yesterday that they were crawling round the floor and tugging at her ankles. The boys were very different in temperament. 'Harry is dark and very sweet. He's sensitive, romantic and he's already got a little girlfriend whom he adores,' she explained. 'Jack is a bit of a Jack-the-lad. He's very blond and stocky and if he can kick your ankles, he will. He loves to scream and shout and throw himself into mud and if he can talk about poos and bottoms, then all the better.'

As a result of working on *Ready Steady Cook*, Fern had to admit that she had managed to learn a few tricks in the kitchen. On a lazy Sunday afternoon, she would often pull a cookery book off the shelf and flick through recipes with the kids. Jack and Harry loved baking. They especially enjoyed measuring out flour and cracking eggs... although they did seem to end up with more of the mixture on their clothes than in the mixing bowl. But over time Fern noticed an improvement – they would even suggest adaptations to recipes! 'The strange thing is I think they're going to turn out to be better cooks than me,' she joked. 'They helped me make some cakes the other day and told me to put some Smarties in the mixture, and they were wonderful.'

As it turned out, Fern could have done with their expertise when Christmas finally arrived. Left to her own devices in the kitchen, she caused a catastrophe. 'I did the same thing this Christmas as I do every year,' she grinned, bowing her head in shame. 'I cooked the bloody turkey with the giblets in!'

Fern hoped her own children would leave home with some cooking skills. As a little girl, she had picked up hardly anything. Her signature dish was beans on toast!

Thankfully, in recent years things had changed. 'I used to be a boil-in-the-bag merchant,' she laughed, 'but things have improved since doing the show.'

Given the trauma of recent months, Fern appeared to be in remarkably good spirits. It was only when the subject of her former husband came into question, that a hint of bitterness was detectible. Commenting on her culinary Christmas conundrums, one journalist queried, 'Your husband must be pleased about that?' Fern responded with a wry smile, 'Yes... when he gets home to taste it.'

By all accounts, Fern's moods still swung like a pendulum, alternating between vibrant happiness and aching sadness. To make matters worse, her divorce coincided with a period of deep reflection, as Fern had turned forty the previous year. Looking back over her life, she wondered where she might be heading next. Was this it for her? Had her one chance of love been and gone? Overall, she felt she should not complain. At least she had three wonderful children and a fantastic career.

In a bid to deal with middle age, Fern agreed to pose for a series of revealing photos in a shoot for the normally prim and proper *Family Circle* magazine. She was photographed wearing nothing but a pair of fishnet stockings, a fake fur stole and a seductive smile. At a voluptuous size sixteen, she decided to celebrate both her age and her body. The public was divided: while some people gasped, others commended Fern for her confidence. Rather than hide her body beneath tent-like clothing, she had chosen to celebrate her natural beauty and admirers queued up to pay their compliments. Here was proof that sexiness did not necessarily equate to skinniness.

'I get fed up with the idea that big women can't be sexy,' she complained. 'Why is it that some skinny women find big women so threatening? Is it because we're voluptuous, that when we take our clothes off we actually look rude and exciting?'

Over time, Fern had learned to love her body and to celebrate her curves. Whereas once she had tried to hide her breasts, now she showed off her ample cleavage with pride. 'I can't understand why there is such a trend towards having silicon bosoms but when you have real ones, they are not valued,' she complained. 'It's that thing of "Oh dear, you've got real bosoms, cover them up."'

Fern was under no illusion that she would ever have what society deemed to be a 'perfect' figure and if the truth be known, she did not really want one. For the first time in years, she felt satisfied with her lot. In the past, she had always loathed her body shape, but looking back at old photographs she was surprised by how slim she had actually been. 'I have photos taken years ago when boyfriends used to tell me I had a chubby bottom. I look at them now and think, "What were they talking about, I was gorgeous!" The problem was, I didn't appreciate how I looked then. So I've decided to make the best of how I look now. That's why I want my photo taken by a top photographer because I reckon with make-up and good lighting I can still look pretty good.'

Of course, there were times when Fern wished she could be thinner. Doesn't every woman! But she came to the conclusion that worrying about weight was a waste of time. She was lucky enough to be able-bodied and felt that she should learn to appreciate the assets she was born with. There would always be someone slimmer, always someone prettier, always someone more intelligent – that was something her mother had taught her. Envious thoughts would only breed negativity. She was much better off being happy with her lot.

'I hope I've got a healthier attitude,' she told friends. 'Otherwise you can screw your life up. Enjoy today, is what I feel: enjoy it. I could walk out of here and get run over by a bus and lose my legs. And then I'd think, "Oh, I liked my legs." Well then, like them today for God's sake!' she fumed.

From past experience, Fern also realised that complaining about being overweight only drew attention to the fact. The reality of the situation was that most men loved her curves. What they hated was the constant complaining! Ex-boyfriends had taught Fern to make the most of the beautiful body she was born with. Wishing she were anything different was disrespectful not only to herself, but also to those who loved her. Now Fern wanted to share that revelation with women in a similar situation. 'It's very unattractive, people going on about themselves,' she complained. 'It's so dreary. I can't be doing with that. I just want to get on with life. It doesn't matter if I'm a size twenty-six, or a size six, I don't care.'

However, her defiant outburst was swiftly followed by an amusing admission. Stepping down from her feminist soap-box, Fern had to confess that there were still occasions on which she did care about her weight. After all, she was only human. 'I do, but I don't care,' she smiled. 'I do, because I'm a woman and you think, "Ooh, I've got to put my swimsuit on." I think we would all like to be a size eight but it is not always possible, so I think it's important to be confident about the way you look,' she said. 'Of course, I'd love to be slim and look devastating in a bikini. But you have to be happy how you are and I am pretty much. This figure is the only one I've got, so I'm going to be happy with it. When skinny women take their clothes off they don't look very sexy, so they aren't scary. But women who've got real curves and lumps and bumps seem to frighten people. Well, maybe I frightened a few people when I did those pictures, but I'm very pleased I did.'

While most female celebrities might deal with a divorce by going on a crash diet, Fern refused point-blank. She would never live her life according to trashy women's magazines. 'Absolutely not!' she laughed. She had never followed so-called slimming tips. Whenever journalists asked her to comment on diet regimes she would always erupt in fits of laughter. 'If I had a slimming tip, I'd be thin! How about "DON'T EAT"? Ha ha! What a bore. People spend their lives doing this "Hunger is my friend" nonsense. It's ridiculous. Life is too short.'

Instead, Fern continued to top up her shopping trolley with all her favourite treats. 'Jaffa Cakes and Cadbury's Chocolate Fingers are always in the house!' she grinned. Her biggest indulgence, however, was 'bacon sandwiches and whisky'.

'Soft bread, butter and very crispy bacon, and a cup of tea with a tot of whisky,' she said, closing her eyes and salivating at the thought. 'At 9.00 am, it sets you up for the day, if you've been working all night.' During the days when Fern was working as a stage manager, it had been her only salvation.

Although Fern felt comfortable with her weight, that did not mean to say that she was completely complacent about her looks. Quite the contrary, in fact! Though she scorned diets, she confessed, 'But that's not to say I won't do everything in my power to hold back the tide of age. I don't want to suddenly turn into a bag lady!' Compared to other women her age, though, Fern had nothing to worry about. Make-up artists would frequently comment on the youthful condition of her skin and most would have put her age at ten years younger. Following in the footsteps of her mother, Fern applied face cream religiously day and night.

The only thing that did bother Fern about her weight was that most clothes stores never stocked larger sizes.

While on a shopping trip with friends as a young woman, Fern was horrified to discover most high-street stores did not stock anything beyond a size fourteen. It was as if fashion had forgotten the larger woman. The only clothes in her size tended to be frumpy and unflattering. Holding several of the garments up to the light, she would turn to her friends and then collapse into fits of laughter. It was ridiculous. After visiting the third shop in a row, however, her patience started to wear thin; it was no longer a joke – just a pain in the rear end.

'What does upset me is when I go shopping for clothes,' she fumed. 'You walk into the shop and there's nothing to fit you. And they look at you as if you are clearly a freak. They say, "We've got this nice tent here." No, I don't want a tent, thank you!'

Fern could not understand it. Why weren't larger women allowed to look sexy as well? 'Bigger women have fantastic bosoms, they've got great bottoms, they've got everything to show off!' she exclaimed. 'Women with bits and pieces look great. But when you see those make-overs on television for bigger women, they put them in bloody awful trouser suits, with big flappy legs, long jackets and a tent top underneath. All concealing. Why are they so scared to let a woman show her womanly body?'

Thankfully, Fern found a fashion sanctuary in high-street stalwart Marks and Spencer. She could constantly be heard singing the praises of their comfortable clothing and stylish diffusion lines. At least they refused to discriminate against size! 'I love Marks because you can find clothes to fit you!' she exclaimed.

Fern despised the way bigger women were represented in the media – it was something that had always bothered her since her early days of working in television. Television studios were often bustling with pretty young things the size of a matchstick and the camera could be cruel, but people's snide, backhand comments tended to be worse. 'On television there's either the standard blonde or the big fatty, the big, big, big fat woman. But there's nothing for the ordinary woman who walks around in Marks and Spencer's.'

On one occasion, Fern even went to the lengths of having an outfit custom made by the haute couture fashion designer Vivienne Westwood. It was an extravagant purchase, but at the time Fern felt like spoiling herself. She described it as 'a BIG Vivienne Westwood number I had made for me. It's so gorgeous, with a boned bodice in a bluebell colour'. Fern had selected the shade in honour of her little daughter. An habitually frugal woman, Fern is still astonished by the amount of money she paid for the dress. 'It was well over the top and cost me far too much!' she laughs. But it was worth it! Not wanting the garment to go to waste and collect dust in her wardrobe, Fern even kindly loaned it out to friends. Several months later, Fern ran into Vivienne Westwood and gushed about how popular the dress had been. 'I met her and told her that both my twenty-three-year-old nanny and my seventy-four-year-old mother looked great in it. She was thrilled!"

In all honesty, Fern's wardrobe had never been her main priority. She had far more important things to worry about and admitted, 'I'm not very focused on how I look and what I'm wearing. I'd much rather be living in the world and enjoying it.' In fact, Fern blamed most of her bad press on the unsuitable clothes she was forced to wear for work. She had always been a jogging bottoms and baggy T-shirt kind of a girl. Trouser suits and smart blouses were completely incongruent to her character. 'I always look better in jeans and a scruffy T-shirt,' she insisted. 'People always say, "Cor, you look nice." It's when I'm done up to the nines in my bloody working suits, which are not me, that I get the most criticism.'

As a woman in her early forties, Fern could happily make light of her fluctuating waistline. In many ways, it gave her a sense of character and identity. 'When I walk into a room, I always feel as if I'm the Queen Mary who has just docked, surrounded by tiny little tugs,' she joked. 'I feel huge, sailing in with all these tiny people all around me.' It was Fern's ability to discuss difficult topics with such ease that made her instantly likeable. Unlike many of the stick-thin blondes who paraded across the television screen, there was nothing threatening about friendly Fern. The public loved her. She was one of them.

People also admired Fern for her self-confidence. Despite working in one of the most body-conscious industries, she still managed to hold her head up high. But it had not always been that way. Fern had experienced her fair share of self-loathing. 'I have felt despair in the past. I've gone through those times – don't ask me when, because I can't quite remember – but I know that I have gone to bed at night and thought, "Oh, please let me be a good girl tomorrow. Please let me eat sensibly. Please don't let me just throw chocolate biscuits down my throat. Please let me lose two stone overnight.'

Thankfully, those days were long gone and Fern no longer felt the need to stick a padlock on her biscuit tin. No longer in denial, she comfortably ate as much as she wanted. As it turned out, by refusing to restrict herself, she actually ate less. Fern left the diets to everyone else; she had found her own niche. She was a loving, caring maternal type with an underlying sex appeal. 'I am a bit mumsy, because I am a very maternal person,' she admitted. But Fern would hate to be pigeonholed as a dowdy, middle-aged frump. Although she was prepared to poke fun at herself, that did not automatically make her a door mat. No one had the right to look down on her.

'What I do find is that some women – and I do like women very much – a small section look at me and think I'm fair game. They think I'm naïve, jolly hockey sticks and someone they can ridicule. And they underestimate me badly.' A case in point involved an incident in a television studio.

Fern was sitting in the green room, filling in time until

her next studio recording. She was flicking through a magazine, when another well-known female presenter walked in. Fern glanced up and smiled, but the other woman completely blanked her. Slightly embarrassed, Fern returned to her reading material. Several minutes passed, and then Fern decided to make herself a cup of tea. Being polite, she asked the other woman if she would like anything. Without bothering to lift her head, she simply grunted a 'no'. By now Fern was incensed, but she refused to make a scene. Instead, she sat calmly at the other end of the room.

Almost two hours passed before the woman finally looked up and acknowledged Fern. Staring at her intently, she narrowed her glare and then a wave of recognition washed over her. Fern tells the story: 'Suddenly she said condescendingly, "Oh, don't you do that Ready Steady F***?"' Fern was shocked. Not wanting to create a scene, she simply smiled and calmly corrected the woman, pointing out that the show was currently one of the most popular programmes aired on daytime television. 'What was her problem?' fumed Fern afterwards. 'I think some people think bigger means stupid. Easily dismissed. At their peril!'

She was absolutely right. *Ready Steady Cook* had been hailed as one of the BBC's most successful shows, and Fern had every reason to be proud of herself. In fact, much of the show's popularity was attributed to her bubbly personality. At the Good Food Awards that year,

Ready Steady Cook was even named Best Cookery Programme. 'I'm absolutely chuffed!' beamed Fern. 'We won out of seventeen nominees. For the second year running!' If only Fern's old home economics teacher could have seen her then! 'I'm sure lots of people there would have preferred a show that presents food in a more stately way,' she shrugged. It was proof that a good television show need not necessarily be glossy and high brow.

When it came to collecting the award, Fern was ready to savour every last moment. The ceremony was a plush black-tie affair and, on this occasion, Fern was willing to forego her comfy jeans and T-shirts for smarter attire. Finding the right outfit would have been hard at the best of times, but Fern was even more limited by her dress size. Determined to make an entrance, she went in search of a slinky number. Unfortunately, she encountered the usual pathetic excuses from most shop assistants: 'We simply don't stock your size,' they would smile condescendingly. Rather than become despondent, Fern battled on in her quest to find a suitable dress. Almost on the verge of giving up, she stumbled upon the perfect fit.

'It was a wonderful stretchy velvet dress,' she explains. It was exactly the kind of outfit larger women were supposed to avoid. Clinging to every lump and bump, it was a daring statement, and it appealed to Fern in an instant. 'I'm very, very lumpy in it, but you know, I don't care.'

Attempting to be diplomatic, the shop assistant described Fern as rounded.

'No, I look lumpy!' laughed Fern.

Scurrying off to the back room, the assistant returned with a selection of stomach and thigh supports. 'Perhaps it would work better with these foundation garments?' she helpfully suggested.

Fern flatly refused. In this instance, it was all or nothing.

'I had to wear a bra, otherwise they're down to my knees!' she laughed. 'But anything else? I didn't want to.'

Instead, Fern decided to make a feature of her curves. Hiding beneath layers of elastane would have amounted to embarrassment and denial. This was her body and she was proud of it. So, when the night of the awards ceremony finally came around, she defiantly decided to let it all hang out. 'All your thighs splurge out at the side, and it rolls over the top of your waist,' she joked to a friend. In a bid to avoid the dreaded VPL (visible panty line), Fern even opted to go commando! 'It was no knickers for me!' she confessed. 'No tights and no knickers. Thank God it was a warm night.'

By all accounts, *Ready Steady Cook* was a runaway success. Fern had even discovered a love for cooking – a chore she had always hated. During one production meeting someone happened to mention what a great idea it would be to publish a recipe book. Members of the public were always writing in to request recipes and, given her fan base, Fern was the ideal person to front the project. Initially, Fern had her reservations. A complete kitchen novice up until a few years previously, it seemed ridiculous that she should be competing with the likes of Delia Smith and Jamie Oliver. But the producers convinced her that it was a great idea. She would be the complete antithesis to the expert gourmet: someone down-to-earth, to whom normal people could relate.

Eventually, Fern agreed and her book *Fern's Family Favourites* was published in March 1998. Written with the cook and home economist Susie Magasiner, the book featured sixty recipes alongside tips on preparing food for the busiest of people. Fern confessed that Susie had been responsible for most of the creations. 'Of the sixty recipes, twenty are mine and forty are Susie's,' she revealed. 'But in terms of cooking we're on the same wavelength. We both have children and like to cook quick and easy things.'

As predicted, the book proved to be extremely popular. A year later, in October 1999, Fern followed it up with a second book, *Winter Treats and Summer Delights*.

Despite her many achievements, it had been a difficult year for Fern. Physically, she felt drained. She had barely had time to recover from a difficult pregnancy before having a new set of challenges thrust upon her. Life as a single mother was hard and, emotionally, this had been one of the toughest periods of her life. The end of her marriage to Clive had left Fern extremely distraught. She hated to give up on anything, but in this instance they had simply reached the end of the road.

Fern came to the conclusion that she needed a break.

'As you get older, having kids leaves you weary,' she explained to colleagues. On the advice of her mother, Fern decided to take a holiday. She had friends in Hong Kong that she had been meaning to visit for some time. Invigorated by the idea of foreign travel, she booked her flights. 'I'm escaping for four days to visit friends in Hong Kong,' she told reporters. 'I'm looking forward most to the BA flights! Sitting on my own, eating, drinking, watching the film, sleeping.' At that particular moment, it sounded like bliss! Unlike most celebrities, however, Fern shunned business class in favour of bog-standard economy. 'I was going to upgrade myself, but do you know how much it is? £3,500! So it's goat class for me.'

Slowly, Fern was becoming accustomed to her new lifestyle. Rather than dwell on losses, she chose to celebrate her fortunes. She had three healthy children and a fantastic career. What's more, she had the love and support of an entire nation behind her. Albeit for one piece of the jigsaw, her life was complete. But very soon that too would slip into place. Fern was about to find love a second time around.

Chapter 5

A Surprise Romance

Alongside its culinary content, the popularity of *Ready Steady Cook* was largely down to the personalities involved in making the show. The team clicked from the first day of shooting and were forever engaged in humorous banter. Because most of the chefs involved had outside commitments, they worked on a rotational basis. Although Fern was familiar with all of them by sight, she was not so good with names. One particular chef, who always seemed to slip her mind, was a handsome young man called Phil Vickery. While women in the audience were drooling as much over his good looks as his fantastic food creations, Fern did not even bat an eyelid.

'When he first came on the show I wasn't aware of his presence and I couldn't even remember his name!' she admitted. 'Who's in today?' she would ask producers on arrival at the studio. They would run through a list of names and, when they came to 'Phil Vickery', Fern drew a blank. Furrowing her brow, she thought hard. Suddenly, she clicked. 'Oh yeah, the one who looks like a dentist!' she exclaimed. She was referring to the fact that Phil had a habit of rolling up the sleeves on his chef's whites. For some reason, he reminded Fern of a worker in the medical profession. 'I always thought he looked like a dentist or an osteopath, because he always had his sleeves rolled up in his chef's whites,' she later explained. 'But apart from that, I never paid the slightest bit of attention to him.'

For his part, Phil had always been fond of Fern. It was hard not to resist her charm! 'I liked her,' he admitted. 'She was good fun and friendly and happy and nice.' Fondness, however, soon turned to fancy. 'After a couple of years working with her, I would look at her and think, "You're quite a sexy old bird," but, as far as I knew, she was happily married and off limits.' Resigned to admiring from afar, he simply put his head down and got to work.

Despite the torturous pain and agony she was experiencing inside, Fern had done a great job of concealing her marriage break-up from her colleagues. At work, she always appeared bright and bubbly, but it was all a front. Fern could not bear anyone to know the truth – that would entail admitting the reality to herself. Instead, she would do her crying in private. No one had a clue. 'There were times when I'd go into my dressing room and burst into tears,' she admits. 'Then I'd mop up and go and do a show. Superficially I was OK, but looking back I don't know how I managed to keep up the illusion. I'm rather amazed that I could switch from "down" to "up" so convincingly, but I suppose if you've got mouths to feed at home, you go out and do the work.'

But Fern could not keep up the front forever. Things came to a head when Fern and the gang were asked to present *Ready Steady Cook* at the Good Food Show in Birmingham. It had been a particularly hard day. Tossing and turning in bed the night before, Fern had hardly slept a wink and, to make matters worse, Jack had a stomach bug and had been playing up non-stop for the past two days. She hated to leave her children at home when they were unwell. They were in safe hands with her mother, but Fern still felt guilty.

Having started the day on a back foot, things did not get much better. On public display, Fern was under pressure to be her usual smiley self. Tired and irritable, she had had enough. On a number of occasions, she nipped off to the toilets to have a weep. For the most part, no one noticed...except Phil. Watching from a distance, he noticed that Fern was far from her usual self; she seemed unhappy and distracted. Biting the bullet, he wandered over to check if she were OK. Red in the face and clenching her fists, quite obviously she was not. Putting his hand reassuringly on her shoulder, Phil whispered, 'You need a glass of champagne, girl.'

'I was having a horrendous time,' said Fern, recalling that day. 'My marriage had collapsed a while ago and I was so tired. I was low and things at home weren't good. He came up to me and asked if I wanted a glass of champagne. I thought, what a nice bloke you are and what I really need is a cup of tea. But a glass of champagne would do very nicely, thank you.'

The pair sat down in a secluded corner and Fern emptied her heart. 'She told me her husband had left her and we talked for ages,' says Phil. The pair had never really spoken before, but Fern instantly felt comfortable in Phil's company. She proceeded to offload her problems and felt as if a great weight had been lifted from her shoulders. Phil listened patiently. Once a married man himself, Phil had also been through a painful break-up. He blamed the split on 'working long hours, paying the mortgage and growing apart'. He sympathised completely with Fern's situation and tried to offer the best advice he could. There was no easy solution, but Fern appreciated his kind words of consolation. 'We sat down, had a drink and talked for half an hour about bits of life that had been happening to us,' Fern recalled.

On the way home that evening, Fern thought about her conversation with Phil and smiled. She was not sure exactly why, but his company made her feel warm inside. What a nice young man the dentist had turned out to be! But it was nothing more than a passing thought. As she neared home, all her other problems came flooding back and Fern was far too preoccupied with her home life to think of anything else.

'I didn't really see him again for six months, and I forgot all about him.' said Fern. Phil, on the other hand, could not stop thinking about Fern. A flame of attraction had been ignited and it was difficult to ignore. Gently simmering at first, it grew stronger by the day. Phil was biding his time; he knew Fern needed space. She was coming to terms with a difficult marriage break-up and that was no easy process. Playing the gentleman, he took a step back and waited patiently for the right moment.

A break in filming meant that the pair would not cross paths for some time. When they did finally meet again, Phil was amazed by the transformation in Fern. Smiling and relaxed, she almost seemed like a different woman. Time had clearly done her plenty of favours. With her marriage break-up firmly behind her, she seemed to be moving on with the rest of her life. Eager to catch up, Phil invited her out for a coffee and, recalling how great their last conversation had been, Fern happily accepted his invitation.

Phil asked how Fern had been coping in the past few months, but the conversation quickly steered away from marital breakdowns to far more optimistic topics. Phil talked about his house in Somerset and spoke of his blissful weekends. 'I had a wonderful morning,' he smiled. 'I took the dog out over the hills.' Although he had been single for some time, Phil had learned to love his own company. He enjoyed nothing more than rising early and taking a stroll through the fields. The air was so crisp and fresh and it was a million miles from the hustle and bustle of London. Despite being a sociable person, he valued solitude and loved his quiet life. Of course, he would love to share it with somebody one day, but for the time being he was happy.

Fern was impressed. It was an idyllic image, as Phil said, 'On the weekend I'm going to go out for a walk.' It was exactly the sort of world she had always dreamed of inhabiting. She admired Phil's contentedness with life – it was almost contagious! 'What's this lovely young man doing just walking his dog?' she thought to herself. 'I'd like a piece of that life.' A seed of attraction had been firmly planted in Fern's mind. 'I thought he was rather nice and that was it!' she smiled.

Although Phil had an inkling that Fern might be interested, he was still uncertain as, winding up another pleasant conversation, the pair went their separate ways. Over the next few weeks, they both thought about each other. Convinced that nothing would happen, Fern had quickly banished any thoughts from her head – it was just a silly schoolgirl crush. Now into her forties, Fern had resigned herself to being single for the foreseeable future, since any man entering her life would be taking on a great challenge. Although she was now much happier, Fern was still prone to the odd bout of depression. Together with three demanding kids and her unsociable working hours, it was not the greatest package around. Besides, she also had her children to think of. Her days of casual dating were long over; these days she was only in the market for a serious relationship and her main priority was to provide her children with a stable home life.

'I decided that to inflict children on anyone, or anyone on the children, just wouldn't be fair,' she admitted. 'It had been a difficult time for all parties concerned and I didn't think I would ever find anybody else, at least not until the children had grown up. I had been on my own for a year before I met Phil and I was expecting to be on my own for at least another ten years. I said to myself, "Forget it, Fern. Get on with your life and be happy with the kids." I don't get lonely and I wasn't scared about being on my own. But I didn't know what was around the corner.'

Phil was equally quite content being single: 'Before we started seeing each other, I was quite happy being single,' he shrugged. 'But I suppose love happens when you least expect it.'

For the next few weeks, Fern and Phil only saw each other during filming for *Ready Steady Cook*. They always said hello and engaged in the odd bit of banter, but gradually both parties realised that they were becoming friends. As the season drew to a close in March, plans were made for a wrap party at London

Zoo. The event would also mark the 500th show. Given the show's success, it was tipped to be a lavish affair. Fern planned her outfit carefully. She might be a mother in her forties, but she could still look drop-dead gorgeous on a night out and even her kids remarked on how long she was taking to get ready! With so many responsibilities at home, Fern rarely had the opportunity to go out these days. Whenever a window did become free in her busy life, she was determined to make the most of it. Having applied her make-up, she stepped back and examined her reflection in the mirror. 'Not bad!' she chuckled to herself.

When Fern arrived at the party in Regent's Park, she was greeted with a flute of champagne, and she was impressed. The place had been decorated to the nines and no expense had been spared. Waiters were weaving through the crowds with silver trays of canapés balanced precariously on their shoulders and a host of tantalising smells filled the room. Fern could not resist sampling a few of the nibbles on offer. After all, she had to line her stomach for all those wonderful cocktails.

In a room filled with familiar faces, Fern felt instantly at ease. It was great to kick back and relax with her colleagues on a non-professional basis. While in conversation with one of her producers, Fern glanced over to see Phil in another corner of the room and her heart skipped a beat. She was suddenly taken aback. Admittedly, she had had a few drinks and was feeling a little more relaxed than usual. Smiling, she waved. Phil caught her eye and waved back. He also felt a sudden knot in his stomach.

In truth, he had been admiring Fern from afar for quite some time. After weeks of agonising indecision, he had reached the conclusion that he should make a move. Tonight seemed the most appropriate occasion. But, on arriving at the party, he had been struck by a sudden loss of confidence. What if he had misread the signs? What if Fern was simply being her usual friendly self? Perhaps any supposed attraction was nothing more than a figment of his imagination. Hovering in the background, he ran over his options. The least he could do was to speak to her. Knocking back a few more glasses of champagne, he suddenly found the courage.

'I was a bit drunk!' he now admits, slightly bashful at the memory. 'Actually, I was plastered!'

Noticing that Fern was standing alone, he seized upon the opportunity to speak with her in private. It was now or never!

'You look fantastic,' he told her.

'Thank you,' said Fern, now a little nervous herself.

There was a moment's silence. There was nothing for it. Phil simply had to cut to the chase and tell Fern exactly what was on his mind.

'I'd had a few drinks, so I said to her...well, I can't repeat what I said to her!' he laughed. 'Let's just say it was along the lines of "I quite fancy you".'

'Do you mean that?' asked Fern, wanting to check this was not just the drink talking.

'Yes I do,' he replied without hesitation.

Fern smiled to herself. She would wake up tomorrow and wonder if this had all been a dream.

'What do you kiss like?' she smiled now flirting outrageously.

'I don't know actually,' grinned Phil playfully. 'Why don't you come outside and find out.'

Checking that the coast was clear, the pair sneaked outside. It was a warm night and the air was heavy with expectation. Gazing at Fern, Phil took a minute to admire her flawless skin, illuminated by the moonlight. She was an incredibly beautiful woman. He must be the luckiest man alive. As their lips touched for the first time, he experienced a wonderful feeling of elation. It was a moment he wished would never end. 'It was lovely,' he smiled, still savouring the memory.

Eventually, the pair managed to tear themselves away.

'So,' said Phil, breaking the silence. 'Do I kiss OK? Or does it need working on.'

'You'll do just fine,' winked Fern, bashfully playing cool. If she were being honest, it was absolutely amazing. For a moment they held each other's gaze and it was only when they heard the sound of voices close by that they decided to return indoors.

When the party finally ended, Fern and Phil said an awkward goodbye. Although they were both desperate to share another passionate kiss, the opportunity simply did not present itself. There were too many people around. Fern was just too damn popular! Instead, Phil took a cab back to a hotel. The next morning, he awoke with a very sore head. Lying back in bed, he tried to piece together his evening. Suddenly, he remembered his encounter with Fern. 'What have you done, you bloody idiot!' he sighed, clasping his fists to his forehead. How on earth would he ever face Fern again? What must she think of him? He must have come over as such a lech. He cringed at the memory of his chat-up techniques. She would probably never speak to him again. Now he had really blown it.

As for Fern, she woke up with a great big smile on her face. Even the children noticed she was unusually upbeat that morning. She was so excited that she even managed to forget about her hangover! Retracing the events, she still could not understand how it had all happened. Twelve months ago Phil Vickery had been the chef who eerily resembled an osteopath. Now he was a potential love interest. 'I thought, "Golly, that was interesting!"' she said.

As filming had finished for the current series of *Ready Steady Cook*, it would be some time before Fern would see Phil again. This time she was not prepared to wait another six months. Picking up the phone, she dialled the Castle Hotel in Taunton where Phil worked as head chef.

'Hello?' he asked.

Even the sound of his voice sent shudders down her spine.

'It's Fern,' she replied.

There was a long pause.

'I can't talk right now,' said Phil, rather flustered. 'I'm really busy.' And with that he hung up.

Fern was slightly taken aback.

'Oh well,' she thought to herself. 'I suppose he'll ring back when he's ready.'

But it was several months before the couple actually met again. Phil still cannot forgive himself for hanging up on Fern. 'I was such a fool!' he admitted. The truth was, he did not know what to do next. Having been single for so long, he was a little out of practice. In the cold light of sobriety things were a lot harder! And he spent an entire summer agonising over his stupidity.

It was in September 1998, when filming resumed for *Ready Steady Cook*, that Phil and Fern met again. Fern had enjoyed spending the summer with her family and any thoughts of romance had evaporated. But on seeing Phil, she was reduced to a pathetic schoolgirl. She could barely even look him in the eye without blushing! All she could think of was that fantastic kiss! If only she could experience it a second time around. Glancing at each other over a *crème brûlée*, Fern was struck by the ridiculousness of the situation. At one point their hands accidentally touched as Phil reached over for a spatula and her legs turned to jelly.

During the day they barely exchanged a word. 'It was a little awkward,' Fern admitted. But, judging by Phil's behaviour, she was convinced this was not a one-sided attraction. As the day came to an end, Fern decided to break the ice. She asked Phil how his summer had been and he gushed about the beauty of the countryside and reminisced as to how glorious the weather had been. Fern smiled. This was the life she wanted. Checking his watch, Phil realised he would have to move quickly to make his train back to Somerset.

'Don't worry, I'll give you a lift,' offered Fern.

There was no way she was letting him escape a second time. Slightly stunned, Phil did not know what to say. As it turned out, he had very little option. Fern bundled him into the car and drove away. Of course, she had no intention of driving him home.

'I put him in the car and drove him straight to my house!' she laughed.

Phil has his own version of events: 'Then, one night, she kidnapped me in her car, took me home and we've never looked back!'

Over the summer, Phil had come to the conclusion that perhaps he was better off being single. He had a comfortable way of life: 'I wasn't looking for a relationship – I had my own house, a good job, nice holidays and had my dog for company – but was resigned to the fact that I might be on my own at sixty with no kids. It didn't worry me.'

But there was something about Fern that he found completely irresistible.

The next morning, Phil woke up slightly dazed. 'I wondered where on earth I was!' he said.

He searched around for his clothes.

'I couldn't find any of them!' he exclaimed. 'She'd chucked them in the washing machine so I couldn't do a runner.'

From that moment on the pair were inseparable.

Of course, Phil had reservations. His last relationship had left him completely heartbroken and he was reluctant to become so involved with someone again. 'I'd been married before, but it only lasted for two years before my wife left. We didn't have any kids and I haven't seen her since. Having such a bad marriage first time round made me very careful.'

But it was too late. He and Fern were already falling hopelessly in love with each other and there was nothing he could do. Instead, he just had to let go and enjoy the ride.

'Fern turned my life upside down,' he said. 'I do think we found and rescued each other at the same time.'

Fern could not agree more. She was about to embark on the most exciting and fulfilling journey of her life.

Chapter 6

The Perfect Match

Since both had been in serious relationships before, Fern and Phil agreed that they should take things slowly. But it was impossible trying to hide their feelings from other people – especially at work! Very soon the production team cottoned on to the budding romance. But try as he might, Phil could not take his eyes off Fern and at every given opportunity he would brush past her or give her a sly pat on the bottom. Fern always giggled to herself. It was hardly discreet!

They need not have worried. Aside from the odd bit of teasing, everyone was pleased for the couple. 'I did get a bit of light-hearted ribbing from the chefs,' Fern admitted. 'Especially Antony Worrall Thompson and Brian Turner! They were always mentioning Phil to try and embarrass me.' Fern was not really that bothered, though. 'It's all done with a sense of humour,' she grinned.

But everyone agreed that Fern and Phil made the perfect couple. Why hadn't anyone thought of setting them up before? Fern had been through a tough time over the last few months and she deserved some happiness in her life. 'It is no secret how much in love they are,' revealed one crew member. 'They can't hide how much they feel for each other.'

As for Fern, she still could not believe what was happening. If anyone had predicted the romance twelve months earlier, she would have laughed it off as preposterous. 'I wasn't looking for anyone,' she insisted. 'I'd had a year on my own and I wasn't looking for love. I didn't want to meet anyone. And I definitely didn't think anything was going to happen. I just wanted to concentrate on bringing up the children, keeping them safe, secure and happy, and that's the end of that. And I was quite prepared to do that. I was happy and enjoying myself in no particular manner and was calm. But there he was out of the blue and the chemistry between us was instant.'

While most rule books would advise against relationships in the workplace, in Fern and Phil's case it proved to be a major advantage. Clashing work schedules had caused problems in both their past relationships. Now, they could spend as much time together as possible. Fern could not believe how well everything was slipping into place.

Alongside the TV show, the couple were also involved in a *Ready Steady Cook* national tour. They visited forty different theatres around the country, including High Wycombe, Derby, Nottingham, Leicester, Cambridge, Cardiff and Fern's old stomping ground, Southampton. It was a punishing schedule, but Phil was always on hand to make sure that Fern was well looked after.

'He makes sure there is a cup of tea for me when I arrive, even takes the shoe trees out of my shoes and then, when it is time to move on, he packs everything up for me!' she gushed.

Fern loved being on the road – every show was a completely different experience. The idea was to replicate the television series on stage, but all the ingredients were purchased from local supermarkets and cooked in a specially designed kitchen. A huge video screen was erected above the stage, which took seventeen crew members five back-breaking hours to assemble. Fern always felt sorry for the crew members; not only did they have to lug heavy equipment around all day, but they also had to do all the mounds of washing-up each night! Still, at least they got to eat meals cooked by a team of celebrity chefs. It wasn't all that bad!

'We had a rock 'n' roll crew with all their big trucks looking after us!' she laughed. 'They usually go out with Madonna and Robbie Williams, and I said, "Sorry, it's only us, we're going to ruin your street cred." But, by the end, we were great mates!'

By the end of the forty-day tour, the crew estimated that they would have got through 600 eggs, 100 pints of milk, 50 pints of cream, 100 bottles of wine, 150 lb of butter and 300 cloves of garlic. That was some shopping list! But if Fern had any concerns about putting on weight, they were quickly set to rest. Thanks to her exhausting schedule she was using up more calories than she could actually consume!

The tour played to packed houses in every town. Fern was delighted by the warmth and sincerity of the audiences. Her fan base was massive and she found the response completely overwhelming. Several hecklers would often interrupt the show by asking Fern whom she was dating, but Fern would simply glance at her colleagues and start laughing. 'Good on you, girl!' screamed one woman.

More than anything, Fern was amazed by the amount of attention that the male chefs received. 'You wouldn't believe the female adoration which surrounded our younger chefs,' she gasped. 'In Basingstoke, the audience was virtually all women and it was like they had come to see the Chippendales. If the boys had gone into the audience, they would have been torn from limb to limb.'

Of course, Fern could understand exactly where they were coming from. Had she been in the audience, she, too, would have been clambering to grab hold of Phil's chef's whites. 'There can't possibly be anything more attractive than a man who can make you fantastic food, can there?' she winked.

Although being on the road was fun, Fern hated leaving her children at home. She missed them desperately and insisted on returning home to see them every night. 'Being on the tour is fantastic,' she smiled, 'but the downside is being away from my children. I drive home every night wherever we are to make sure I am there for them.'

Phil was in awe of Fern. Her commitment to her family was really admirable; she would move mountains to see her children. 'I have promised them a fantastic holiday and ice creams every day after I have finished the road show,' she told Phil. And it was statements like that which made him love her even more.

Her children were extremely understanding; they had grown up with the show and it had naturally become a big part of their lives. 'I had already given birth to the boys when I started presenting it and was pregnant with Grace, so even my children have grown up with it!' smiled Fern.

Now Phil had become a fixture in the household, the picture was complete. 'He is very much part of our lives,' said Fern. So, without wishing to tempt fate, she could safely say that her life was panning out perfectly. Whereas past relationships had been a struggle, life with Phil was stress-free. 'Phil had been divorced for a long time when I met him and has no children of his own which obviously made our situation less complicated,' said Fern.

Some friends even joked about how incestuous the situation had become. They commented that Fern would forever be connected to the show. 'My best friend said to me the other day that I was always going to be known as Fern *'Ready Steady Cook'* Britton!' she laughed. 'Well that's fine by me, because I'm very proud to be associated with it.'

Very quickly, Fern realised that she would be with Phil for the long term. For the sake of her children, however, she resisted temptation and took things slowly. Although she would have loved for Phil to move in immediately, both agreed that it would be better to wait. As it was, Phil spent most weekends with Fern anyway and there was no point in adding any unnecessary pressure. Fern did, however, feel confident enough in the relationship to make it public. The news instantly made tabloid headlines. It was a classic tale of romance. Fern Britton was the nation's darling and everyone wished her well. This was one story that deserved a happy ending.

'I have never spoken about this before, but yes – it's true. I am very much in love!' she told one newspaper. 'Phil is a wonderful man and I want to spend the rest of my life with him. He is gorgeous and kind and everything I could ever wish for in a man and I am deeply in love with him.' The tabloids were filled with pictures of Fern looking bright-eyed and deliriously happy.

The couple had grown extremely fond of each other in a very short space of time. Fern could not imagine what life would be like without him. She did not even want to entertain the thought! Instead, she imagined a future brighter than she could ever have conceived of in the past: 'I have this vision of me in twenty years' time in a lovely sunny drawing room with French windows wide open and vases of lupins on the piano and children and dogs running about on the lawn. And, yes, I hope Phil is a part of that, too.'

'I love everything about him,' she continued. 'The way he speaks to me, the way he makes me feel and the way he treats me. Not only is he gorgeous, he is so loving and kind. It is the little things he does for me that mean so much.'

At home, Fern and Phil were content with each other's company. Rejecting industry parties in favour of walks in the countryside, they led a normal and peaceful life. It was absolute bliss. From very early on, they both realised that their goals in life were identical: happiness. Neither could ask for more. 'Off stage, we are both quiet people who are just in harmony with each other,' said Fern.

Fern even took the plunge by cooking for Phil! Admittedly she was nervous; even though she had picked up a few skills on the show, she was by no means a gourmet chef. Knowing her limitations, she stuck to something simple. That morning she had woken up before Phil. Wide awake, she decided to get out of bed and do something useful. 'Shall I make breakfast?' she asked Phil. Still half-asleep he mumbled something that resembled 'yes'.

Up until then, Phil had always done the cooking. He was so talented in the kitchen that Fern did not like to interfere! But after a while, she started to feel guilty. Often Phil would arrive at the house tired from a long day in a hot kitchen. The last thing he felt like doing was switching the oven on. There was no way she could compete with his creations, but he would appreciate the gesture.

She opened the fridge and for a moment felt quite daunted. There were so many weird and wonderful ingredients, but her eyes settled on a carton of eggs. She could not go wrong with those! When Phil finally managed to climb out of bed, he was greeted with a waft of home-cooking smells. Following his nose to the kitchen, he found Fern scraping viciously at a frying pan with a spatula. 'Sit down!' she demanded. Dutifully, Phil obeyed her orders.

'I'm not much of a chef, but I have cooked for Phil which was a brave thing to do. He'd never had anyone cook for him before and I thought, that's not right. So I cooked him scrambled eggs on toast,' recalls Fern. 'I put the plate in front of him and barked, "Eat it!" He ate every bit and said it was lovely!'

He wasn't even lying! As any chef would agree, food always seems to taste better when cooked by another person. The fact that Fern had cooked it made it taste even better!

'Chefs love it when you cook for them!' beamed Fern. 'So now I do. Beans on toast, he's happy. Ready-made gravy granules, oh wonderful. Waffles, frozen, in the toaster with an egg on top, he loves the whole lot.'

However, Fern was willing to extend her repertoire. As time progressed, Phil shared a few cooking secrets of his own. Even before getting together with Phil, Fern had been fond of men who could cook. She had always maintained that a man who could perform in the kitchen also inspired passion in the bedroom. 'Cooking has become far more sexy,' she once revealed. 'Take chef Antonio Carluccio. He's the most gorgeous bloke. I'd love to put my key in the lock and he's in the kitchen knocking food up and pouring a glass of wine.' But she was quick to add, 'His wife is very nice too!'

When quizzed about her comments a year later, Fern blushed with embarrassment. 'Did I really say that?' she exclaimed in disbelief. 'Well, I do believe it,' she said after a brief period of thought. After all, her relationship with Phil was living proof of the fact: 'I have always believed that men who can cook are way ahead of the game in terms of pulling power.'

But cooking was not the only interest that Phil would spark in Fern. He was a keen motorcyclist and loved to whisk Fern away on his bike. She would ride pillion as he zoomed down country lanes on retreats to Dorset or Somerset. It was a thrilling experience and Fern felt like a giggling teenage girl. She had very little experience of riding a bike and the whole idea felt quite rebellious. It also gave her an excuse to grip tightly onto Phil.

But very quickly, Fern developed a burning desire to be in the driving seat. Bitten by the bug, she decided to purchase her own bike, a 500cc Honda. It was a beautiful piece of machinery and Fern took great care to maintain it. She loved dressing up in leathers, putting on a crash helmet and hitting the road. She felt completely anonymous. If only people knew it was Fern Britton beneath that Evel Knievel outfit! It was a liberating feeling.

'If you'd told me a few years ago that one day I'd be riding a motorbike, I'd have laughed,' she confessed. 'But here I am and I love it. One of the great things about it is that with your hair tied back and all that gear on, nobody recognises you, which is lovely.'

Although Fern had been on numerous bike rides with Phil, her first real taste of motorcycling solo came much later with a new BBC series called *Danger – Celeb At Work* in 2001. Each week two well-known celebrities were presented with the challenge of fulfilling an unlikely job. A camera crew would follow them to track their progress. Fern was given the job of presenting the show and was even the subject of the final programme. She was given the task of working as a motorcycle dispatch rider down in Brighton. 'Although [at that point] I had never ridden a bike, it was my idea,' she said. 'I thought it was a challenge.'

Unfortunately, Fern's learning curve was not quite as swift as she had imagined. She was not about to give up her day job! 'I fell off the bike and was useless as a courier,' she confessed. 'But it was fantastic fun. It inspired me to take my test and, to everyone's amazement, I passed first time!'

Neither Fern nor Phil could believe that they had found each other. Some people waited all their lives for a love like this and still never found true happiness. Phil's friends and family were deeply impressed by his choice of partner. 'When we first got together, I phoned my dad to tell him,' said Phil. 'There was a pause and he said: "You lucky sod." And when I told my younger brother he said: "Are they real?" – a reference to Fern's ample bosom – and I said: "Oh yes. Very real!" She is the best thing that ever happened to me.'

Fern was equally in awe of her new boyfriend. All her friends congratulated her on the relationship. Her mother, Ruth, thoroughly approved. Fern kept wondering when her luck might change, but it never did. 'I think he's gorgeous!' she swooned. 'He has so many good friends. To find a man who has genuine friends is a good yardstick.'

She was right. Phil was extremely popular and had a reputation for being a good listener. People would often come to him with their problems and he was always happy to offer advice.

On one occasion, Fern even came home to find him weeping with one of his friends. Arriving home she found the house in almost total darkness. 'Phil?' she called – she could have sworn that he was staying in for the night. Then, in the distance, she heard a gentle sobbing. She stopped and listened closely. It was coming from the living room. Walking over, she noticed that the door was slightly ajar. There was a faint beam of light from a desk lamp. She eased the door open slightly. There on the sofa was Phil, and next to him was his best mate. Both were red-faced with their eyes puffy and swollen. 'What are you doing?' she asked.

Phil explained later that they had been discussing world politics and the subsequent impact on their children's generation. Fern felt a warm glow inside. 'He's discussed things with his best friend and they've been in tears with each other,' she revealed. 'He's got a lot of female qualities!'

In time, Fern would also be a beneficiary of those counselling qualities. She had warned Phil that life with her would not always be easy because she was weighed down with emotional baggage from her first marriage and still had a lot of issues to work through. But Phil was willing to take on the challenge. In fact, he was more than glad to be of help. Although, for the most part, Fern was deliriously happy, she was still prone to debilitating bouts of depression and at times she had absolutely no control over her emotions, and that frightened her. Even though Prozac had helped her in the past, she had been warned that the depression might return: 'With depression, something takes you over and you just want to turn the lights out. You can smile, but inside you're shrivelling. You wake up and feel as if you can't get out of bed. But you force yourself to get up and think, "Can't people see that I'm in agony?" It is so physical you think other people must be able to see it. But if you try to tell anyone there's something wrong, they just say, "You? Oh you're always fine."'

For a while, work proved to be her only salvation. On set, she demonstrated that appearances could be deceptive. 'It was a difficult time,' she said. 'I was so grateful for my job because there were moments I could come to work and turn into that other person. I could take a big Fern Britton pill as I call it, and get dressed up and turn into this other person. It was lovely; I could step out of myself. It was my saviour. People expect you to be the person with no problems on the show, so fine. Often when I am at my most smiley, laughing out loud and being a pain in the arse, is when I am the most unhappy. And the calmer I am and the less I am smiling, I am much happier.'

But with Phil, Fern no longer had to pretend. He knew her too well and instantly recognised when she was not feeling herself. Some days he would find her sitting alone and staring into space. It was always her eyes that gave the game away: she could greet him with the widest smile, but when her eyes had lost their twinkle, he knew that something was wrong and he would wrap his arms around her tightly as if shielding her from the world outside. Fern had never felt so safe in all her life.

'I don't know how he coped with me,' she has admitted.

'I was all fine and dandy on the surface but underneath I had an awful lot going on.' At her lowest points, Fern even considered suicide. 'If I wasn't such a coward, I know I would have killed myself,' she said. 'I definitely contemplated it.' One particular occasion sticks firmly in Fern's mind. It had been an extremely tiring day, as that morning she had been up at the crack of dawn to start filming in the studio. Little Grace had been crying all night and Fern had been tempted to call the doctor out. She could barely pull herself out of the front door and the sky was a depressing grey colour, which did little to lift her mood.

In the car on her way to work she began to dredge through a tangle of painful memories that were usually shoved to the back of her mind. Feeling weak, she was unable to keep them at bay and as the day wore on her depression became almost intolerable. No matter where she turned, there was no escape from the oppressive torment. Even though she had been down this road before, it did not feel any easier. If only, just for a minute, she could switch herself off.

On several occasions, Fern thought about phoning Phil. But as she went to dial his number, she was overcome with a sense of futility. He would probably be busy in the kitchen at work and she did not want to disturb him. Once home, she decided to run herself a hot bath; that might at least offer her a little comfort. Then she could close her eyes, go to bed and wake up to a new day. She ran a handful of bath salts under the hot tap. The sudden sweet fragrant scent made her feel almost nauseous. Slipping into the bath, she closed her eyes and tried to block out the day.

Suddenly. she was struck by an horrific thought. Darting round the bathroom her eyes settled on the medicine cabinet. 'I remember sitting in the bath thinking, "How many pills have I got in the bottle?"' she recalls. Thankfully, that moment she heard Phil turning his key in the door and instinctively she cried out to him. Throwing his coat to the floor, he ran to her aid. 'If it hadn't been for Phil, God knows what would have happened.'

'Everything seemed to come to a head,' she sighed. 'I was so low. Even remembering it now makes my eyes well up. It's a horrible feeling and you can't really explain it to anybody. You think to yourself: "I've got everything, so why do I feel so miserable?" But you can't help it.'

Emotionally, Fern felt trapped and she was unable to share her torment with the rest of the world. Today, however, she has no problem discussing the matter. If anything, she hopes that her experience might help others in a similar situation. 'I don't think there's a stigma attached to owning up to something like that,' she shrugs. 'People are so much more open nowadays – and it does help. I can quite understand how people can say, "I had dinner with him last night and he was fine." Then the next morning they are found hanging dead.'

'You just have to accept that depression is mostly

chemical and not due to the fact that you are mad, bad or anything else. Once you have sorted that out in your head you can get help.' Thankfully, that is exactly the course of action that Fern decided to take. 'I felt so much better,' she said. 'A line has been drawn and I'm through it.'

But Fern accepted that she would never fully be rid of the 'disease'. Over time she would simply learn to cope with her mood swings and to identify the causes. 'Depression is with you always,' she said matter-of-factly. 'It comes and goes, but as you grow up with it you start to recognise when it's arriving. I used to be very good at seeming all bright on the outside so that people had no idea how I felt inside. But now, if I feel a depression coming on, I just allow myself to feel bad and wait for it to go away.'

During these periods of unhappiness, Phil was extremely patient. Fern later described him as 'her rock'. In retrospect, the couple believe that Fern's problems brought them even closer together. One thing was certain: Fern knew Phil would stick by her through thick and thin. Here, she had found a companion for life.

Top: Fern Britton in her element, presenting live television to the nation.

Bottom: In addition to *This Morning*, Fern has also hosted a number of high-profile programmes, including *Soapstar Superstar*. Here she is pictured with winner and *Coronation Street* actor Richard Fleeshman.

Fern's rapport with guests and viewers alike is never stronger than when larking about on set with Phillip Schofield (*top*) or candidly discussing the naughtier things in life, like sex toys with sex expert Donna Dawson (*bottom*).

Fern's engaging and professional interview technique means celebrities and politicians beat a path to the *This Morning* sofa. She is as comfortable talking with Tony Blair and Princess Anne as she is with Julie Andrews or abuse survivor Stuart Howarth, whose story particularly moved her.

Fern's popularity means she's a frequent guest on the nation's chatshows. Here, she is pictured with Phil on *The Paul O'Grady Show*, sharing a joke with Jane Fonda, Tommy Lee and Vince Neil in the green room of *Friday Night with Jonathan Ross*, chatting to Ant and Dec on their *Saturday Night Takeaway* and being interviewed for *Today with Des and Mel*.

Fern loves an excuse to get dressed up and prove that you don't need to be a size 10 to feel good about yourself!

© Empires/REX Features

Fern had resigned herself to living alone as a single mother before she met Phil Vickery on the set of *Ready Steady Cook*. Her life completely changed the day they started dating, and from the off he has been her greatest champion. The strength of their love for one another is clear for everyone to see.

Radiant with confidence, Fern arrives at the 2005 *TV Quick* Awards with Phil Vickery.

Proud of her achievements in life, Fern Britton is Britain's most enviable star. © Empics

Chapter 7

Family Man

One of Fern's main concerns when she started dating Phil was that he would fit into her family life. It was very important that her children would feel comfortable around him and vice versa. She knew that walking into a household of three kids was a daunting prospect and she did not envy Phil's situation in the slightest! But any concerns she might have had were quickly laid to rest. With typical calm, he breezed effortlessly into their lives and settled in immediately.

Even though Phil had no children of his own, he quickly warmed to Fern's offspring. He had so much energy and, much to their delight, he was always willing to play with them. The twins were now six years old and Grace was three. Fern had to admit they were definitely a handful! But Phil could more than manage. 'Inflicting your children on other people, or other people on your children, is a very difficult thing. But Phil has taken to it like a duck to water and the children are very fond of him,' said Fern.

Phil had no intention of wading in and taking their father's place. He simply wanted to embrace his new family. Fern introduced him as 'Phil' and that is how the children got to know him. At first, they were a little shy; Grace even darted behind Fern and gripped hold of her skirt, but Phil soon managed to coax her out. 'They know he's just Phil and he's not trying to be anything else,' smiled Fern. 'They have a very good father and Phil certainly isn't trying to replace him. But he is able to do things with them that I can't.'

Fern was referring to Phil's rural upbringing: 'He's very countrified and will take them out on walks.' Jack and Harry loved learning about the great outdoors, and Phil taught them how to tie knots and various other handy tricks. Before setting off on an outing, he would always make sure they were well prepared. Both boys had their own walking boots and a compass. As a special treat, Fern even gave them a few biscuits for the journey. She would stand at the gate and wave them off as they ventured down the country lane.

On one such walk, the boys spied a pheasant darting across the path. 'Look!' squealed Jack, pointing at the startled bird. 'That's a pheasant,' Phil told them. 'They taste great in pies!' Switching into stealth mode, he showed them exactly how to catch a pheasant. He was an old hand at this sort of thing! Once he had captured and killed the bird, he even showed them how it should be plucked. On another occasion, he agreed to take the boys fishing. Impatient at first, they soon got the hang of it. Harry was slightly put off by the wriggling worms, but Phil stepped in and agreed to fix the bait. By the end of the day, both boys could competently cast a line. They would always rush home with their catch and proudly display it on the kitchen table.

During the summer, Phil would spend hours playing with the kids in the back garden. He would help them make dens out of a few branches and pieces of tarpaulin from the shed. Fern had to admit that most of his creations were pretty impressive. Phil showed the boys how to make a bow and arrow from twigs and string, and sometimes they divided into two teams and staged a make-believe battle.

'He has taught them all sorts of things,' said Fern. Gestures like that made Phil even more endearing to Fern. 'I am just amazed to have found someone who makes me happy and looks after me. It is such a surprise because I didn't assume that it was ever going to happen,' she said.

Phil even went so far as to buy his own patch of woodland. Lying in bed one night, he had suggested that it would be great to build tree houses for the kids. It was something he had always dreamed about as a child.

Climbing trees was an age-old hobby for little boys; the idea of having a fully functioning nest between the branches seemed incredible. Carried away by Phil's enthusiasm, Fern agreed that it was a great idea. 'Phil is an outdoors person,' she explained to one magazine. 'He has just bought himself some woodland and is going to build the children tree houses.'

When Phil and Fern broke the news to the kids, they were overwhelmed with excitement. Grace screeched loudly and threw her arms in the air. Unlike many children their age, Grace and the twins often shunned the television set in favour of playing outdoors. 'The children love living in the country,' said Fern proudly. 'They have a very good life.'

Fern would think to herself, 'You lucky children!' They had the benefit of two fantastic fathers: Phil and Clive were completely different people but they each had their own appeal and never once did Fern pit the two men against each other. The children would always grow up knowing Clive to be their father. Phil was an extra special treat. 'Between their real father and step-father they have these amazing men with completely different abilities and outlooks on life, but two wonderful men as role models,' enthused Fern.

'The children adore him and trust him,' Fern continued. 'He's not trying to replace their father but he gets on with them so well. They are very lucky to have two such good fathers and we are very lucky to have found each other at this stage in our lives.'

Phil absolutely loved his new role as a step-father. 'He turned up and took the kids on with open arms,' said Fern. 'I couldn't believe how wonderful he is with them.'

Although Phil had no children of his own, he had been brought up to have great respect for the family unit. 'He comes from a very strong, family-orientated background,' Fern explained. 'He's the middle of three boys and his parents were devoted to their sons. They always did things together as a family, so he is very family-minded.'

Fern fully understood his commitment to the idea of family when the household experienced an unexpected power cut one night. All of a sudden, while Phil was helping Fern to prepare dinner, the lights went out. Grace screamed; it was always eerily quiet in the countryside and she was still a little afraid of the dark. Fern always put her to bed with a nightlight. 'It's OK!' said Fern stroking her little girl's hair. 'It's just a fuse.'

'I'll go and check the fuse box,' offered Phil, rummaging around in the kitchen drawer for a torch. But on inspection, he realised that there must have been a power cut. 'Looks like we may be without electricity for the rest of the night!' he shrugged.

There was only one thing for it: they would have to light the house the old-fashioned way – by candlelight. Fern had stashed several candles in the pantry for just such an emergency as this. None of the kids had been bathed yet, but Fern was not about to let them jump into bed without a wash. Phil lit several candles in the bathroom and the couple set to work bathing each child in turn. Grace soon forgot about her fear of the dark. Splashing water and scattering soapsuds about the room, they were having a great time. 'We were having such fun!' giggled Fern. Covered in bath foam, Phil turned to Fern and said, 'Now this is what I call family life.'

Fern will never forget the first Christmas she and Phil spent together. Ever since she was a little girl, Fern had always loved Christmas. She would begin preparing weeks beforehand and would lie in bed dreaming about what Father Christmas might bring her that year. Unfortunately, there were times when she received very little. But Fern nevertheless had good memories of the day.

In recent years, Christmas time had been tough for Fern. After Clive had left, it served as a reminder that her family had fallen apart. 'There were a couple of Christmas Days I had alone with the kids,' she lamented. 'Or I shared them with their father.' Reading festive cards addressed to the estranged couple left Fern with a lump in her throat. Lugging the Christmas tree indoors from the garden, she felt suddenly alone. Never in a million years did she imagine herself celebrating Christmas as a single mother. 'There were some bleak moments,' she admitted, 'though it was tough on him, too.'

Fortunately, Fern's kids did not allow her to dwell on the situation for too long. They loved Christmas time! At least she could always rely on the house being filled with boisterous laughter. Putting them to bed on Christmas

Eve was always a nightmare! They always wanted to wait up and catch a glimpse of Santa and his reindeers.

When Phil and Fern first got together, she could not wait to spend Christmas with her new man. But once again, Fern was left disappointed. Phil had already agreed to work at the hotel in Taunton on Christmas Day and, try as he might, there was absolutely no way he could get out of it. Fern feigned indifference, but inside she felt cheated. Instead, she had lunch with her mother, Ruth. During the meal she managed to keep her spirits up, but on the journey home, she suddenly felt lonely.

'I got back to an empty house and was feeling low,' said Fern. Turning her key in the lock, she resigned herself to an evening in front of the television with only a box of Quality Street for company. 'Then I heard splashing from upstairs and found this gorgeous man in the bath covered in foam!' Feeling guilty, Phil had pulled a few strings and left work early. He knew how much Christmas meant to Fern and there was no way he was going to let her sit at home by herself. Grabbing a bottle of bubbly on the way, he dashed home to surprise her. It was better than any Christmas gift she could have wished for. 'We spent the rest of the day in bed drinking champagne,' smiled Fern. 'It turned out to be lovely.'

After that day, Fern and Phil decided they were ready to move in together. He was already spending most of his spare time at Fern's house in Buckinghamshire and it seemed to make sense. With both their busy schedules and three children to look after, there was barely any free time as it was. The couple cherished every last spare moment that they had in each other's company. Without a shadow of a doubt, Fern had found her soul mate. Their similarities were uncanny: on occasion, they would even finish each other's sentences. Fern smiled to herself – this must be true love.

'Phil and I do get on very well,' she gushed. 'We are similar in many ways. I would rather be with him than anybody else. When I finish working, I really resent the hour and a half I have to spend in the car going home because I want to spend as much time with him and the children as I can.'

Although Phil missed his house in Somerset, the couple agreed to take regular weekend breaks in the West Country. Besides, compared with Fern and the kids, nothing else really seemed that important to Phil any more. In early 1999, he hired a van to transport most of his belongings to Buckinghamshire.

Fern was amazed at how few clothes he owned! At least she would not have to clear too much space in the wardrobe! Although it was a tiring day, the couple were in high spirits. At last, Fern felt as if her life was really shifting up a gear. It did not take long to merge Phil's possessions into the household. Fern remarked on how instantly homely the place looked! It was as if he had been living there for years.

Both exhausted from the day's work, Fern and Phil

collapsed onto the sofa with a bag of good old-fashioned fish 'n' chips – Fern loved eating them straight from the paper bag, doused in vinegar. Both she and Phil agreed they tasted better that way. Holding Fern tightly in his arms, Phil promised that he would stay with her forever. This was the beginning of a new chapter. Smiling to herself, Fern could not believe that it was possible to feel so happy. Surely someone would give her a nudge soon and she would realise that it was all a dream. 'This really is a wonderful time in my life,' she told one interviewer. 'I don't want to sound too slushy, but all I'm saying is that there is happiness around the corner without you even realising it. It's been a wonderful surprise.'

Life at home with Phil was blissful. Even though Fern enjoyed her job, she would constantly count down the hours until she could go home and spend time with her family. In Phil, she had found the perfect match. Not only did she love the man, but she also fancied him rotten. Four years her junior, Fern would joke that Phil was her sexy toyboy. Phil, on the other hand, would wax lyrical about his curvy goddess. When asked by a fan why he didn't prefer someone like Angelina Jolie, he looked baffled and replied, 'Who is she? I don't even know who she is. What does she do? I love voluptuous women. Fern is gorgeous and I love her to bits.'

Working together on the show certainly made life easier for Fern. During breaks, she would always sidle over to Phil for a quick kiss and he could not resist giving her a pat on the bum or a cheeky nudge. It was obvious that the pair found each other irresistible. Usually, he managed to be quite discreet, but on one embarrassing occasion the couple were actually caught on camera!

Phil was preparing a recipe and running through the various ingredients with Fern. Absent-mindedly, he reached over to pick something up and accidentally grabbed Fern's breast. For a moment Fern looked startled and then started giggling. 'Do you mind?' she exclaimed. The entire studio erupted into fits of laughter. Realising what he had done, Phil turned a bright shade of crimson. The recording even made the national newspapers. He would never live this one down! Months later, the television crew still continued to rib him for grabbing 'the wrong melon'.

Even though Phil and Fern spent all day working in the kitchen, they both enjoyed cooking at home. If ever Phil wanted to conjure up a romantic meal, he would always cook lamb chops – 'Fern's favourite'. Returning the favour, Fern would rustle up a cottage pie. 'There's no competition,' grinned Phil. 'It's my favourite.'

Fern liked to do her bit but, for the most part, she allowed Phil to take charge of the kitchen. 'That's one huge advantage of living with a great chef!' she reasoned. 'He cooks everything and never serves up the same thing twice. He makes lovely light pasta dishes and wonderful Sunday lunches.'

But there were disadvantages to having a chef in the

house, too. Any hopes Fern might have had about shedding a few extra pounds went straight out of the window. With so many delicious dishes coming from the kitchen, it was impossible to resist temptation. 'Every so often I try to be a little slimmer and a little fitter but it's not easy, especially with three children and a chef in the house. I don't obsess about my weight!'

The worst was when Phil was working on his recipe book *A Passion For Puddings*. 'Every night I'd get home and there were at least a dozen or so puddings to try!' complained Fern. Each week, he would test out a different treat and Fern was his ultimate critic. Phil would line up several variations of a dessert and ask her to sample each one. If she liked the recipe, it was going in. 'Doughnut week was the worst!' groaned Fern. But her favourite dish was apple crumble. She could not believe how soft and tender the caramelised apples tasted. 'His apple crumble is the best!' she boasted. 'It's just wonderful!'

While Phil encouraged a healthy appetite, Fern was quick to point out that he never forced food upon her. 'He's not a feeder!' she exclaimed, referring to men who love enormously fat women and feed them up to the detriment of their health. 'He's very good. He doesn't shovel it down me. I'm not a goose being fattened up for foie gras!'

Aside from whipping up fantastic creations in the kitchen, Phil also enjoyed relaxing with Fern in front of the television with a glass of wine. Preferring each other's company, they turned down most party invitations. Besides, they did not like to leave the children at home – they were a family now. Most of the time, they liked to watch sport. Phil was a massive Spurs fan and loved to tune in to every game. At one point in his life, Phil even had aspirations of becoming a footballer. 'He's very fit,' revealed Fern. 'He used to run marathons. He's impressed me all round!'

Fern, however, was not quite so keen on the game. 'I can't say I'm mad about it,' she confessed. 'But I'm having to watch quite a lot on TV these days. I'm beginning to cope with it.'

But Fern would get her own back. Bizarrely, she had become addicted to motor-racing. At any given opportunity, she would wrestle the remote from Phil and flick over to the highlights. 'I'm a mad Formula One freak and I can't miss any of the TV coverage!' she grinned. Sometimes, she even checked the listings in the *Radio Times* and crept downstairs in the dead of night to catch a race. She found it extremely therapeutic to watch the cars zoom round the track: 'I love turning on in the middle of the night with a nice pot of tea, knowing the phone won't disturb me.'

Soon after moving in with Fern, Phil knew that he wanted to marry her. If he were honest with himself, he had known since the moment they had kissed in the grounds of London Zoo. But for Fern's sake, he was patient. She had dealt with a lot in the past few years and he did not want to add to her pressures. Besides, the question would hold even more gravitas if he waited. Finally, as Christmas 1999 approached, he decided that the moment would be right to propose.

Searching for the right ring was not too difficult. By now, Phil had a good idea of Fern's style. Female friends had often remarked on his incredible sensitivity towards women's tastes. Everyone trusted his opinion and they even called him an honorary girl! Phil had already showered Fern with several gifts; several months before, he had presented her with two beautiful silver rings as a symbol of his love. Fern also refused to go clothes shopping without her right-hand man; he was even better than her at selecting outfits! 'He takes me shopping and even knows what clothes to choose for me,' she said with delight. 'He's the greatest friend I have ever had in a man.' Phil definitely had a creative streak and a fantastic eye for colour. 'Phil's lovely,' continued Fern. 'He's also very imaginative. He wanted to be an illustrator.'

But it had not always been that way. Phil had made his fair share of shopping mistakes in the past. 'I remember one of the first Christmas presents I ever bought Fern,' said Phil, shaking his head with shame. 'I went into a boutique and bought her some sexy underwear. Being a typical bloke, I managed to get it completely wrong. Fern unwrapped it and said, "These are absolutely gorgeous... If only they were just a couple of cup sizes larger!"'

After much deliberation, Phil settled on a Tiffany engagement ring. It was stunning, and he could not wait to surprise Fern. As Christmas drew closer, he wondered how he should pop the question. Hundreds of romantic ideas whizzed through his head. Perhaps he could take Fern out for a moonlit walk? Maybe he could even splash out on an old-fashioned horse and cart. But none of the ideas seemed quite right. Fern was a down-to-earth kind of girl and had never been keen on extravagant gestures. Besides, with three children running around, it would be impossible to find time alone. And anyway, why would he want to shut the children out? They were as much a part of this love affair. They were all one unit now.

On Christmas Eve, Phil arrived home from work to find the house in chaos. 'It was a typical Christmas Eve,' recalled Fern. 'The kids were running around and I was at the Aga struggling to make mince pies.' Phil smiled to himself. Fern was covered in flour and looked extremely flustered. Even though she found it difficult, she always insisted on making the mince pies. Phil knew they would taste all the better if Fern had prepared them.

Creeping up behind her, he wrapped his arms round her waist and nuzzled his head into her neck. 'I'll cover you with flour!' she giggled.

'Come over here for a minute,' he said gesturing towards the kitchen table, 'I've got something to show you.'

In the background, Christmas carols were playing on the radio. Fern loved getting in the festive spirit.

'Not just now,' she mumbled, while grappling with a pastry cutter.

'That can wait,' said Phil reaching for her arm.

Still, Fern refused to turn round.

'No,' insisted Phil. 'I really think you should see what I have to show you. It's much more important than the mince pies.'

Realising that he would not take no for an answer, Fern dusted her hands and spun round to face him. She gasped in shock. Now down on one knee, Phil was reaching up to her. Something in his hand caught her eye. It was a dazzling diamond ring. Without warning, Fern burst into tears. Overtaken by emotion, Phil joined in. 'We both cried,' said Fern. 'We're a bit soppy like that.'

Fern still laughs at memory: 'I was dressed in a tatty old apron, had no make-up on and the pies were a disaster!'

It couldn't have been more perfect! For the time being, Fern and Phil decided to keep the news to themselves. 'The next morning Phil brought me breakfast in bed with a rose and it was our lovely secret!' smiled Fern. Phil then presented Fern with her second present. Thankfully, it was a marked improvement on his past lingerie disaster. 'It was a brilliant telescope!' said Fern. 'I'd imagined a little brass one, but he gave me this enormous beast.'

Phil had chosen the gift after a conversation with Fern about watching the stars at night. He had a romantic image of the pair sitting outside in the garden staring up at various constellations. Unfortunately, the reality was very different! 'The most interesting thing I've seen is the inside of our neighbours' bathroom!' joked Fern, before quickly adding, 'but that was an accident!'

Burnt mince pies aside, Fern had enjoyed one of her best Christmas Days ever. Glancing at her ring every five minutes, she could not believe what was happening. That night in bed she took a moment to watch Phil sleeping. He truly was a remarkable man. What had she done to deserve this? It did not matter. Whether by fluke or not, he was here now and there was no way she would ever let him out of her sight.

Chapter 8

A Beginning and an End

As they had both had been married before, neither Fern nor Phil wanted to make a great fuss of their union. There was a time when Fern dreamed of wearing a big white gown and arriving at the church in a horse-drawn carriage, but now a little older, she valued her privacy even more. Besides, extravagant preparations would have delayed the couple even further and Fern was impatient to move on with her life. Of course, there were a few legal wranglings to be dealt with, but when Fern's divorce finally came through in February 2000, she was free to marry Phil. Three months later, in May, they went ahead and tied the knot.

Not wishing to create a fanfare, Phil and Fern quietly made wedding preparations. They called up the local register office in High Wycombe and enquired about an available slot. 'We have one free in six weeks' time,' the registrar offered. Phil relayed the information to Fern. Grinning, she nodded enthusiastically. 'We'll take it!' said Phil.

After much discussion, Fern and Phil agreed to keep their wedding a secret; they did not even inform the children. 'We didn't tell anybody!' said Fern. 'It was so exciting having this wonderful secret.' This would be their special celebration. 'We wanted it to be our day,' said Fern. 'We'd been to see the registrar five or six weeks before the date and he granted us a special licence so that nobody would find out.'

Fern picked out some flowers and they both helped each other choose their outfits. 'We even hired a blue Porsche for the day, which was my something borrowed and blue,' said Fern.

Leading up to their wedding day, Fern felt extremely calm. She wanted to spend the rest of her life with Phil and she could not wait to make it official. Fern was old-fashioned and even though she had been through one divorce, she still believed in the sanctity of marriage. But she had never wanted to inflict her views on Phil. Instead, she had kept quiet and waited for him to pop the question. 'I wanted to get married because I believe in a state of marriage,' she admits. 'But I would never have forced Phil's arm. I do have three children and there were complications, so I didn't want him to feel forced into anything. It was so nice because I didn't feel like I was the one making him want to get married,' she smiled. 'He was very keen.'

Phil agreed. 'It was just something we both wanted to do,' he said. 'I thought, "How can any man let this woman slip through his fingers?" When I spoke to my father he said, "You lucky sod!" All my friends were the same.'

'The important thing was that he was very positive about the idea,' added Fern. 'The fact that he wanted to make such a huge commitment – as much as I did – was a lovely compliment to me.'

'On the morning of the wedding Phil took the kids to school so that I could get ready, and on the way back he went past the register office to check if there were any photographers. I arranged for a friend to come over and look after my daughter,' said Fern.

'Why are you taking us to school today?' piped Jack from the back seat of the car.

'Because Mummy is a bit busy today,' replied Phil. 'She has an important meeting to go to.'

Phil caught a glimpse of himself in the rear-view mirror. He could not stop grinning. And who could blame him? In a few hours' time he was about to marry the woman of his dreams. The most beautiful woman in the world!

Phil dropped the boys off at the school gate and waved goodbye. He did feel slightly guilty that they would not be sharing in the celebrations, but there would be plenty of time for a second party. For once, he and Fern deserved to be a little selfish. Driving back past the register office, he checked for any pesky photographers. Even though he and Fern had gone to great lengths to keep their wedding day a secret, there was always the possibility that someone might find out! Fern had a massive fan base and often made headline news. To his relief, the streets were completely empty.

Back at the house, Fern was busy getting ready. After a long soak in the bath, she was carefully applying her make-up. She had woken up with plenty of time to spare; this was one day when she did not want to be in a rush. She thought back to her last wedding day: she had been so flustered, rushing around and making last-minute adjustments. She had been surrounded by interfering well-wishers. Everyone had an opinion as to how she should wear her make-up, what time she should arrive at the church, whether she needed an extra spritz of hairspray. All she had really wanted was a jolly good cup of tea with a tot of whisky.

This was a totally different experience. The house was completely quiet and she felt a wonderful sense of calm. For a moment, she felt a pang of anxiety. 'I was upstairs getting ready and I started to get nervous,' admitted Fern. 'So I switched on the television and Richard and Judy were presenting *This Morning* which calmed me down and restored a sense of normality.'

Closing her eyes, she imagined what it would be like to be Mrs Phil Vickery. Quite damn wonderful, she concluded. 'Are you ready?' called Phil, pushing the bedroom door open. 'Wow,' he gasped, seeing Fern in her full glory. 'You look absolutely beautiful.'

On the way to the register office, Phil could not help glancing over at Fern.

'Keep your eyes on the road,' she giggled. 'You're going to have an accident!'

Once they had parked, they strolled over to the office hand in hand. It was a crisp spring day and the first flowers were starting to open. It certainly felt like the time for a new start. Standing outside the office, the pair turned to each other and smiled. 'Let's do it!' said Fern.

'We simply walked in and got married,' said Fern, recalling the day. 'I was in tears all the way through, and so was Phil.'

With no photographers on hand to take romantic snaps, the couple had brought with them a digital camera. Before the ceremony, Phil had asked the registrar if he would not mind taking a few shots. 'The registrar kept stopping to ask us if we wanted him to take a picture during the ceremony,' said Fern. 'We've now got loads of photographs with rows and rows of empty chairs behind us!'

Before the ceremony, Fern asked two receptionists from the offices upstairs to act as witnesses. Recognising Fern and Phil from *Ready Steady Cook*, they were more than happy to oblige. When Fern and Phil kissed, they even gave them a round of applause! Fern thought back to that first kiss a couple of years earlier; she would never forget that moment. 'Then I handed the receptionists a box of confetti to throw over us as we left,' she said.

After the ceremony, Fern and Phil went for a wedding lunch at Raymond Blanc's splendid Manoir aux Quat' Saisons. So overcome by excitement, Fern almost failed to finish her meal. The whole day had swept past in a dream. Still they did not tell anyone. 'It was only when the phone went on the way back home – somebody asking Phil if he could do some work the next day – that he said, "Not really, I've just got married." Then we went and told my mother,' said Fern. Once Phil had hung up the call, she turned to Phil and said, 'I think we should tell people.' The first person she thought of was her mother, Ruth. But rather than tell her over the phone, Fern decided to do the honours in person.

She arrived at her mother's house nearby and rang the doorbell. 'You look nice!' Ruth said, greeting Fern. Then it dawned on her. 'She took one look at me and she knew,' said Fern.

'Oh my God!' gasped Ruth, clasping her hand to her mouth. 'You've got married, haven't you?' Fern went inside for a celebratory cup of tea and told her all about the day. Of course, Ruth fully understood why Fern had chosen to keep the ceremony quiet. It made perfect sense.

Next, Fern and Phil decided to tell the children. A friend of Fern's had collected them from school and they were back at home. Fern spoke to Jack, Harry and Grace in turn on the phone. She was not sure if they fully understood what had happened, but judging by the excited response, they realised that it was a cause for celebration. 'By the time we got home they had painted us banners and posters which read, "Congratulations Mummy and Phil," and pinned them up on the door,' smiled Fern. Both Fern and Phil were extremely touched. They even re-enacted the wedding for the children. 'I bought them some confetti, and they got to throw that over us, which they enjoyed,' added Fern. Although, for weeks afterwards, she would be cursing herself – there were bits of confetti all over the place! She even found some in the downstairs toilet!

The news spread quickly. Given Fern's feeling about family, some people were puzzled that she had not let anyone else in on the act. But Fern maintained that her kids were too young to really understand what was going on anyway. 'I think they are just too little to have got it,' she reasoned. 'So we didn't tell them what was happening.' But most people understood exactly why Phil and Fern had kept their day so guarded. 'No one minded we'd done it in secret,' she insisted. 'We'd both been married before and had big bashes. What it boils down to is that I really wanted to get married, but I didn't want a wedding. I wanted it just to be us – me and Phil.'

Unfortunately, Fern and Phil had little time for celebration. Within a few days they were both back at work; and quickly slipped back into everyday life. No one would have guessed that they had just exchanged wedding vows. A few days later, their friend and fellow chef, Nick Nairn, came over for dinner.

'It was great to see them at home!' he said. 'I praised Phil's kitchen, helped cook and drank a bottle of Highland Park Scotch as we put the worlds to rights.' It wasn't until later that night that Nick realised his friends were now officially man and wife. 'Next morning I realised I'd just gatecrashed their honeymoon!' he exclaimed.

It was almost six months before the newly-weds could take a proper break. They chose to take their belated honeymoon in North Carolina. It was absolutely blissful. It was a week's holiday with no expense spared. Fern enjoyed escaping from the real world, though she would later confess to desperately missing her kids.

Once back from holiday, Fern and Phil threw a special wedding celebration for all the friends and family who had missed out the first time round. They drew up a list of 100 guests and Fern was determined to pull out all the stops. 'We are doing it properly with a wedding cake, confetti and a children's entertainer!' smiled Fern. The couple settled on Cliveden House in Buckinghamshire as the location. Fern spent days deciding on a design for the cake and Phil recommended a great caterer. It was also very important that the party was family-friendly. Most of Fern's friends had children by now and she went to great lengths to ensure that all the children present would have a great time.

'I'm really looking forward to it!' beamed Fern, just days before the event. 'Because there won't be any emotional pressure. Our actual wedding was very emotional. We were both crying!' Now Fern could sit back and enjoy the party. 'Why doesn't everyone plan weddings like this?' she thought to herself.

Fern and Phil had a fantastic day. Fern had to admit that the entertainer she had hired was definitely the star of the show. Grace and the twins were mesmerised by his repertoire of magic tricks and even Fern was impressed by his balloon animals! The catering team also did themselves proud with a decadent buffet spread. But best of all was the wedding cake! Two little figurines, representing Fern and Phil, had been perched on the top. Feeling sentimental, Fern popped them in her handbag as a keepsake. Everyone was given a slice of the cake – and some people even came back for seconds!

That night Phil and Fern lay in bed giggling about the day's festivities and the oddly-shaped balloon animals now littering their front room. Once their laughter had subsided, Fern looked into the eyes of her new husband. A song sprang into her head. 'For you are here, loving me, whether or not you should/So somewhere in my youth or childhood, I must have done something good,' she sang out loud. Phil racked his brains trying to place the song. 'It's from *The Sound of Music*,' explained Fern. 'It's the one Julie Andrews and Christopher Plummer sing to each other just before their wedding.' Fern remembered the first time she had heard that song – it was on one of those trips to the theatre with her father. Phil pulled Fern towards him and held her tightly. A tear started to roll down her cheek. 'Oh dear,' she sobbed. 'Aren't I the soppy one?' Drying her eyes, she looked up. To her amazement, Phil was crying as well.

As it turned out, married life was even better than Fern could have imagined. 'Even now we look at each other and say: "Are we married?"' smiled Fern. And there was no risk of complacency. Every day, their love for each other seemed to grow stronger. Even though they were man and wife, the pair acted like teenagers discovering love for the first time. 'Not a day goes by when Phil doesn't wake up in the morning and tell me that he loves me.' Gestures such as that made Fern realise that she had made the right decision.

At this point in their relationship, Phil and Fern knew everything about each other. Their lives were totally interlinked and they had absolutely no secrets. 'He has become such a good friend,' said Fern. 'And I find it amazing to have a true partnership with somebody. He knows how to make me happy and look after me. I do the same for him and he will always thanks me.'

One of Phil's greatest attributes was that he never took Fern for granted. 'He is romantic, but in a thoughtful, not a slushy way,' smiled Fern. 'If I'm ill for a couple of days, he will put me to bed, appear with a hot water bottle and tell me not to worry about the kids because he is taking care of them. Or if it's a frosty morning and the car is iced up, he will already have been outside to switch the engine on so that the car is defrosting in time for me to take the children to school. It's kindnesses such as that which are more important than huge bouquets of red roses.'

With three kids constantly running under their feet, maintaining a passionate relationship was not the easiest of tasks, but Phil and Fern still fancied each other just as much as the first day they met. Phil would constantly snatch a sly glance at Fern and she would always grin back in return. In every aspect, their relationship was perfectly fulfilling. They were both deeply in love and passionately in lust. It was a unique and winning combination.

Although Phil and Fern's daily timetable always revolved around the kids, they made sure to factor in spare time for themselves. 'It's very difficult,' admitted Fern. 'But I'm strict about bedtime, so after 7.00 pm we usually manage to sit down on our own, have a glass of wine and watch television together.'

Often, Jack and Harry would refuse to go to bed, preferring to stay up and play in the front room. Fern did not like to shout at her children, but she was quite stern – especially on school nights! If they misbehaved, she would threaten to reduce their pocket money for the week. But most of the time, after much cajoling, they would obey their bedtime curfew. Fern would promise to read them a bedtime story, which always did the trick. A long walk in the country also worked a treat. The fresh air and exercise always guaranteed a good night's sleep.

When the children had been carefully tucked up in bed, Phil would present Fern with a large glass of ruby red wine and the pair would snuggle up on the sofa – and there was nothing Fern loved more! She always looked forward to those cosy evenings in front of the television. 'It sounds very boring but I love it,' she shrugged.

Sunday lie-ins also proved to be a bit of a problem. In a perfect world, Fern and Phil would spend hours in bed reading through the papers with a cup of steaming coffee, but that was rarely the reality. No sooner had Fern turned the first page of her supplement, than a small face would appear peeping round the door. 'Mummy,' Grace would whisper. 'Can I come and sleep with you and Phil?'

It was difficult to say no! Fern would glance over at Phil, one eyebrow raised, before hoisting Grace up and under the duvet. Squeezing in between Phil and Fern, Grace would wriggle and squirm under the covers until she found a comfortable position. Of course, Fern loved her daughter's company, but sometimes she wished for even just an extra half an hour alone with her husband.

Fortunately, Phil came up with a great idea to guarantee some peace and quiet. Fern came home one day to find him sitting at the kitchen table surrounded by pieces of cardboard and a pack of felt-tip pens. It certainly made a change to the usual scene of cooking utensils and fancy ingredients! She laughed to herself – he must have stolen the colouring pens from the kids' playbox.

'What are you doing? she asked.

'Wait a minute!' demanded Phil, shielding his creation from view. 'I've just figured out the perfect solution to our privacy problems.'

Fern folded her arms and stood back. Now she was curious! 'Ta-dah!' exclaimed Phil, having added the finishing touches. He held aloft a piece of card for Fern's approval. 'Vacant,' she read, looking a little confused. He then adjusted it to show a second message: 'Meeting in progress'. Scratching her head, she could not quite figure out the connection.

'Are you planning on holding some sort of conference in the house?' she joked.

'Don't be daft!' sighed Phil, shaking his head. 'I've made them to hang on the bedroom door. This way we'll never get disturbed!'

Fern burst into laughter and came over to give him a hug. 'Phil has a sign to stick on our bedroom door which you can slide across so it says "Vacant" or "Meeting in progress",' said Fern. 'It doesn't necessarily mean anything naughty is going on but it does allow us some privacy.'

Later, Fern went one step further and bought a 'Go Away' mat to place outside their bedroom door. 'But people keep walking over it and ignoring it!' said Fern, bursting into laughter.

Both Fern and Phil credited the success of their marriage to the fact that they had both been involved in serious relationships before and had learned from their mistakes. 'We've had relationships that went wrong – and that was primarily because people get used to each other, stop respecting each other,' reasoned Phil. 'Both of us are now wary of what can go wrong and we're determined not to let that happen.'

'We've both been married before, so we know how to avoid all the usual relationship pitfalls,' added Fern. 'And we just get on very well. We talk about everything, we laugh about everything, we have no inhibitions with each other, we're not scared to say anything. He understands.'

While Fern's personal life was in perfect working order, her professional career was also soaring to new heights. She was in the process of recording a mammoth ninety *Ready Steady Cook* shows and also standing in for Judy Finnegan one day a week on *This Morning*. 'It's a dream job!' she grinned. Ironically, however, Fern was becoming less and less interested in pursuing her career. She would much rather spend her time being a mother and wife.

'I am slowing down,' she insisted. 'I have had to turn down an awful lot of work. It's wonderful to have all that work, but it's so important for me to be with the children. I've got to a stage where I want to be at home with them. I am happier there than anywhere else. The children are my top priority and I think my work is taking me away from them. I don't mind if it means the end of my career. It doesn't worry me.'

Phil and Fern discussed the matter at great length. Fern desperately wanted to scale down her work commitments and Phil was willing to support her. With only one breadwinner in the house, they would inevitably have to make changes to their lifestyle. But for the sake of her children, Fern was willing to make cut-backs. She had successfully demonstrated that it was possible to juggle motherhood with a professional career, but now she wanted to concentrate full time on her kids. The last thing she wanted was to look back and wonder how her kids had grown up so quickly. She did not want to miss a minute of their development. Every day, Jack and Harry seemed to grow a little taller, and Grace was starting to use longer words. This was her real life. No amount of money could buy that experience.

After much deliberation, Fern decided that it was time to call it a day on *Ready Steady Cook*. It had been a fantastic few years and she owed a lot to the show. Not only had it helped boost her profile, but it had also introduced her to the love of her life. But she had come to the end of the road and it was time to move on. She had presented over 1,000 shows during her career to a total audience of sixteen million. That was quite some achievement! When Fern broke the news to her production team, they tried desperately hard to make her stay. But no amount of persuasion would make Fern change her mind. Eventually, they bowed to her wishes and agreed to let her go. Celebrity chef Ainsley Harriott was appointed as her replacement. No one envied his position; Fern was a hard act to follow! 'I'm extremely grateful to Fern for handing over *Ready Steady Cook* to me,' he told one journalist. 'But she didn't tell me just how much hard work was involved in making the show!'

'It wasn't a five-minute decision to give up,' she pointed out. 'It did take me a year to decide. But I have been so mad with work and other commitments that I don't feel I have been as absorbed with my children as I used to be. I want to enjoy a normal life with them. As it is, I worry that they think everyone goes off to work in a chauffeur-driven limo because cars arrive for me and they think that's the norm. That's why I drive them around in a Mini. And I think that if I can be there for them, then they will have more normality in their lives.'

Fern continued to present *This Morning* one day a week with John Leslie and she also stood in for Richard and Judy while they were away on holiday. But she admitted to having few major ambitions left to pursue. 'I've never been very ambitious,' she confessed. 'But I'm lucky to have worked non-stop for nearly twenty-one years. I have enough of an ego to think that I would like to keep going, but there is nothing I feel I haven't done.'

'I have taken such a step backwards this year and my wages have gone down accordingly,' she continued. 'So I'm very happy for Phil to be the major breadwinner now. I'm just happy doing my job and earning a crust. And if it all ends tomorrow, I would be quite happy to go and work in Marks and Spencer.'

Phil and Fern had budgeted carefully and, according to

their sums, they could survive quite comfortably. Neither of them went out much and life in the countryside was simple and cheap! Fern had never had a habit for extravagant purchases, preferring to stick to her trusted M&S wardrobe. 'We've got enough for fish and chips and a bottle of wine without thinking,' she joked. 'But not a world cruise for the whole family.'

Unfortunately, however, not everything went according to plan. For the past few years, Phil had been juggling various television appearances with his job as head chef at the Castle Hotel in Somerset. But as his television career took off, he found himself more and more in demand. Naturally, he had a commitment to his workplace and struggled hard to marry the two careers. Inevitably, though, the pressure became too much. Personnel at the Castle Hotel were unhappy with the increasing number of hours Phil was devoting to television work and it was suggested that Phil was putting his television appearances before his work at the hotel. Eventually, his superiors called him into the office for a meeting and dismissed him on those very grounds.

Phil was furious and extremely upset. He arrived home and broke the news to Fern, but there was little she could do to console him. She did, however, agree that the accusations were extremely unfair and unnecessary, and, most likely, they were the result of pathetic jealousy and bitterness! Phil had always been extremely devoted to his work at the Castle Hotel and had gone out of his way to ensure that the kitchen ran smoothly.

An industrial tribunal case ensued. Even though Phil eventually won, it was a difficult period for the family. Phil resented having his integrity questioned and found the whole incident extremely humiliating. On many an occasion, Fern would arrive home to find Phil at the kitchen table with his head in his hands. He was usually so calm and collected and she had never seen him this upset. Although Phil was never outwardly angry, he generally walked around with a dark cloud over his head. The whole experience affected Fern and for a while her bouts of depression returned.

'Even though I won the case, it left a bad taste in my mouth,' sighed Phil. 'It was just sordid and needless. I was angry with the injustice because I'd done nothing wrong. The irony of the whole thing is I'm still a shareholder and there's nothing they can do about it.'

On Fern's advice, Phil decided to set up his own business and work for himself. By now he was a household name with great contacts in the industry. As well as writing recipe books, he set up his own company, and never once did he consider returning to work as a hotel chef. 'I did that for twenty-two years and it was time to move on,' he concluded. 'I've set up a new company, which does consultancy, development, demonstrations and publicity stuff.'

Now working mainly from home, Phil could spend more time with his family and Fern was delighted. Once again, life was fitting perfectly into place. There was only one drawback – Phil insisted on doing all his recipe preparations at home. Pudding days were torturous. But Phil also had a habit of using bizarre ingredients. On several occasions, Fern walked into the kitchen to find pieces of offal draped on the kitchen table!

'Phil used to have his own restaurant but now he works for papers and magazines, as well as on television,' explained Fern. 'All his recipe developments are done at home, so we have his and hers fridges! His always has horrible things such as liver, kidneys, trotters and tripe, while mine contains nice girlie things like yoghurt and fresh juices!'

Now Phil and Fern were working mainly from home, their household seemed livelier than ever! Some days, it seemed as if the place were bursting at the rafters. As the kids grew older, they were accumulating more and more stuff and Fern was running out of storage space. Both she and Phil had started to entertain the idea of moving to a bigger property. Much as she loved her house in Buckinghamshire, it seemed a little too small for a family of five. For the time being, Fern felt unable to make a decision, but in the end, her hand was forced. Fern and Phil were about to welcome a new addition to the household.

Chapter 9

Baby Number Four!

Before meeting Fern, Phil had little knowledge of fatherhood. With no children from his previous marriage, he had resigned himself to the fact that he would probably never be a parent. But all of that changed in an instant, and he happily embraced Fern's children as his own and learned quickly on the job. However, he had always harboured a desire to have a child of his own. To Fern's surprise, he eagerly suggested the idea very early on in their relationship.

Fern understood his position and she desperately wanted to have a child with him as well. But there were several logistical problems. Now in her early forties, Fern was reaching a dangerous age to give birth. She also had the matter of her fibroid to contend with. Her pregnancies had been progressively more painful and she dreaded to think what might happen the next time around.

Most importantly of all, however, Fern wanted to give her relationship with Phil space to grow. Rather than rush into having another child, she wanted to enjoy falling in love. She was also extremely old-fashioned and did not wish to have a child out of wedlock. 'Phil was all for trying for a baby right away but I wanted to do things the right way around,' Fern pointed out. 'When Phil and I first got together, I used to say to him that he was young enough to have children. But I'm very old-fashioned and didn't want to have a child without our being married at that stage because I wasn't divorced. We knew each other for about eight months before we started living together and then my divorce came through and we were married three months later. I'm glad we waited.'

Once they were officially married, Phil and Fern started trying for a baby almost straight away. They were both desperate for a successful result. 'We did have a few false alarms,' admitted Fern. 'My period would be five minutes late and I would think, "I must be pregnant!" and then we forgot all about it.'

But there was no rush. 'We thought if it doesn't happen, it doesn't happen,' added Phil. 'But it was something we hoped for.'

Fortunately, they did not have to wait too long. The following Christmas, Fern and Phil received their best gift ever! During Christmas dinner, Fern noticed that she was feeling quite queasy. 'Is anything the matter?' asked Phil, as Fern stumbled into the kitchen clasping her stomach.

'Oh, nothing,' she replied. 'I've probably just eaten one too many chocolates!'

'Go and sit down,' said Phil putting one arm around her – using the other hand to stir gravy. 'I'll look after the cooking.'

Several days later, Fern still felt a little abnormal. She had her suspicions but did not want to raise Phil's hopes unduly. Instead, she went to Boots and bought a home pregnancy test kit. At the time, she and Phil were out in town picking up a few bargains in the January sales. The crowds were ridiculous and on Phil's suggestion, they decided to seek refuge in a nearby café. 'I'm just going to the toilet,' said Fern, looking unusually furtive. 'Could you order me a cappuccino?' Phil paid for the coffees and sat down in a window seat, waiting for Fern to return.

'We were having a coffee in a little café. I nipped off to the loo and did a test – he didn't even know I'd bought one,' said Fern. 'I came back and said, "I've got something to tell you."'

Phil looked up from his newspaper to see Fern grinning from ear to ear. 'What's the matter?' he asked, confused by her sudden happiness.

Unable to speak, Fern simply opened her hand and showed him the test strip that she had been clasping. It took Phil several minutes to register exactly what was happening. 'He spluttered his cappuccino all over the place!' laughed Fern. 'It was our best-ever present.'

The news came as a great surprise to Phil. 'We had so many let-downs, false alarms,' he shrugged. 'You think it's not going to happen.'

Fern agreed: 'It's miraculous it did happen. Amazing!'

Initially, Phil suggested that they should keep the news a secret, but he could hardly contain his excitement. Within hours, he was on the phone breaking their good news to friends and family. 'He said: "Let's not tell anybody," and then proceeded to tell every single person!' giggled Fern.

'We were so excited!' she continued. 'No one could take the thrill away from us.'

Phil was in his element. He could not stop smiling for weeks afterwards. 'I was over the moon!' he exclaimed. 'I've never had any children. Both my brothers have kids but I never really thought it would happen to me. I'd almost resigned myself to being a single bloke. Then, within three years, I met Fern, got married and now we have a baby!'

Phil and Fern agreed that they must be living out a fairy tale. 'It does, really does,' insisted Phil. 'Over the past couple of years, we've both had rough times one way or the other and it's just lovely to come out of it.'

Ever since Phil had first raised the topic of having a child, it had become a major focus for them. He desperately wanted to become a biological father. Not wanting to pressure Fern, he tried to play down his feelings – the last thing she needed was a nagging husband! But Fern knew how much Phil wanted a baby and each false alarm came as a major disappointment. 'We'd been trying for a baby for about a year,' she said. 'I kept telling myself it wouldn't be a problem if we weren't able to have a child. After all, I had three children already. But I wanted one for Phil. Even though he's brilliant with my three and sees them as his own ready-made family, I wanted him to experience fatherhood.'

In the early stages of her pregnancy, Fern suffered the usual bouts of morning sickness. Phil would frequently find her doubled over in the bathroom. Opening the fridge, she suddenly felt sick when staring at certain foods. 'I was sick virtually every day,' she complained. 'I wasn't like that with my other pregnancies – it's a Vickery thing.'

At forty-three years old, Fern's age posed potential problems for her pregnancy. Doctors advised her to take several tests to ensure her that unborn baby was perfectly healthy. She had refused to do so in the past, but on this occasion Fern agreed it would be a good idea: 'I didn't start having children until I was thirty-six and I'd always refused the checks. This time I thought, for all of us concerned, we'd find out whether things were all going according to plan.'

On the day of the tests, Fern felt slightly apprehensive, but Phil was by her side at all times, squeezing her hand tightly. To their relief, doctors gave them the all clear. 'We had the test and she [the baby] was fine,' confirmed Fern.

But the final two months of Fern's pregnancy were extremely difficult. One evening, Phil came home to find her crouching in the living room. Clutching her sides, she was wincing with pain. 'What's wrong, Fern?' he asked with alarm.

Her body was contorted and she seemed out of breath. Counting down slowly, Phil helped her gain control of her breathing. He hated to see his wife in this state and was deeply concerned that something might be wrong with the baby.

'I'm going to call the doctor,' he said, reaching for his mobile. Within half an hour the doctor was ringing the front doorbell. Fortunately, by this time, Fern's pain had subsided slightly and she was able to sit up and sip a glass of water. After giving Fern a preliminary examination, the doctor suggested that she should make an appointment to see her gynaecologist. He could not be 100 per cent certain, but he had a hunch that the problems were being caused by a fibroid on the outside of Fern's womb. The benign – but painful – tumour had been aggravated by the hormones released during pregnancy.

After giving birth to Grace, she had been warned that the problem might recur if she were to fall pregnant again. And until now, Fern had convinced herself that she had more or less escaped, but the shock of the sudden pain reminded her of the agony she had been through with her previous pregnancies. She was not sure if she could cope a third time round. Gripping her hand, Phil reassured his wife that he would support her all the way, and that made a massive difference.

After a second consultation, Fern's fears were confirmed. A fibroid was indeed the cause of her excruciating pain. This was just something she would have to ride out. Even though it became familiar, the pain never grew any easier to deal with: 'Every night I'd be on all fours in the living room, trying to get some ease – but it just didn't happen.'

Phil would frequently drive Fern to the hospital when the pain became too much to contend with. Light-heartedly, she would joke to nurses that she was becoming something of a regular. Eventually, doctors put her on pethidine, a powerful drug normally used during labour. Fern recalled that she was in a tremendous amount of pain, far worse than anything she had experienced during her last pregnancy. This time round, she described the pain as 'incapacitating'. Her fibroid had grown to a much larger size than ever before. 'It grew to the size of a golf ball!' she winced. 'At times, you could see it sticking out of my tummy.'

'It was agony,' said Fern. 'There was one large one which they couldn't take out because there was a risk of haemorrhaging which could have endangered me and the baby. I was in the most excruciating pain I have ever experienced in my life. I felt so rough towards the end. I can't tell you how bad it was. Even talking about it now makes me want to throw up. I was in and out of hospital for the last two months of my pregnancy.'

Despite struggling with a difficult pregnancy, Fern miraculously managed to continue her one-day-a-week commitment to *This Morning*. Phil suggested that she should remain at home full time, but Fern refused to let people down. Instead, she soldiered on. But in the later stages of her pregnancy, Fern found herself dashing back to her dressing room more frequently: 'I felt so ill with the persistent, constant pain.' Things came to a head when Fern suddenly collapsed in the studio. Phil recalled the moment: 'One day she had to lie on the studio floor, she was so ill. They had to get someone else in.'

Struck by a sudden and shooting pain, she fell to the floor and crumpled into a heap. Members of the crew instantly ran to her aid. 'Fern, are you OK?' they asked. For several moments, Fern could barely speak. Several people tried to help her up, but she seemed incapable of moving. Every time she shifted an inch, the shooting pains would return. Fifteen minutes passed and by now people were starting to grow concerned. Eventually, Fern managed to lift herself up onto the sofa. She reached for her script but slumped backwards. The production team looked at each other. Fern was in no fit state even to stand up, let alone record the show. Everyone agreed that she should go straight home and rest for a few days.

'We're going to send you home, Fern,' instructed her

producer. Nodding her head, Fern agreed. All the way to her house she feared that the unbearable pain would return. Fortunately, she made it back in one piece. Her mother, Ruth, was waiting to greet her. She rushed over to the car and helped Fern clamber out. 'You're going straight to bed!' she declared. Once indoors, Fern felt much better, but she was exhausted and within a matter of minutes she had drifted off to sleep.

By now, Fern had become a regular fixture on *This Morning*. The British public loved starting the day with her happy smile and cheerful banter. Producers had noted that over time, Fern's fan-mail bag had grown substantially larger than any of her colleagues'. Typically, Fern took it all in her stride. As far as she was concerned, the husband-and-wife team of Richard and Judy were the real stars of the show; she was merely cast in a supporting role.

Even though Fern enjoyed presenting *This Morning*, she had absolutely no inclination whatsoever to increase her workload. 'I was very happy to stay at home and be a housewife and mother,' she said. 'I took it easy and didn't miss the work at all!' Every day she would get up and prepare breakfast for the kids and by 7.30 am the kitchen was a riot of activity. Fern refused to let her children leave for school without a proper breakfast. They normally had the option of cereal, porridge or toast – not to mention the obligatory piece of fruit.

Once she had dropped the kids off at school, she would

return home for a relaxing cup of coffee. There were plenty of household chores to keep her busy and she still had various work commitments. When she did have some spare time, Fern loved to sit down and read a book. During her time on *Ready Steady Cook* she had barely been able to turn a page. The only reading she had time for was scripts and production schedules, and Fern valued her free time and did not want to give it up.

Of course, there had been plenty of work offers. 'My agent, Jon, did say to me a while ago: "If in the unlikely event of Richard and Judy leaving, would you like to take over?"' said Fern. 'And I said, "No I couldn't possibly do that."'

But in July 2001, rumour became reality when Richard and Judy made the shock announcement that they were leaving *This Morning* and defecting to Channel 4. Naturally, the producers turned to Fern. For some time, they had considered approaching Fern with more work. As a working mother who had survived divorce, she really appealed to the average housewife.

Much to their disappointment, Fern refused even to entertain the idea. She was six months into her pregnancy at the time and instantly ruled herself out of the running. She had enough on her plate! Taking on a television presenting role five days a week would have been tough at the best of times. She had also made a vow not to take on any major work commitments in the next few years: 'I ruled myself out because the baby was due on 3

September and the show was coming back on 5 September.' Showering her with flattery, the production team tried desperately to persuade Fern otherwise. But she had already made her mind up and adamantly refused. However, as a compromise, she did suggest that they ask again in several months' time. 'I told them I would be available from the New Year onwards if there was still a job going,' she said.

In the meantime, the legendary sixties model Twiggy was taken on as a presenter, along with Colleen Nolan. But viewers failed to warm to the new-look show. As the ratings fell drastically, producers once again turned to Fern. But she was far too preoccupied even to take a phone call. To everyone's surprise, she had gone into premature labour.

At the time, Fern and Phil were sitting at home in bed, relaxing in front of the television. Reluctantly, Fern had allowed Phil to watch the early-morning football highlights. By now, she knew all the rules and even most of the players' names! Funnily enough, she even found the commentator's voice oddly soothing. She had joked to Phil that their unborn baby would probably grow up to be a footie fan.

Then, without warning, Fern let out a yelp. A tea cup slipped from her hand and smashed to the floor. 'Fern?' shrieked Phil, spinning round. He had become accustomed to Fern's sudden bouts of pain and usually knew how to help her relieve the pain. But this time her cries sounded different. He knew something was definitely wrong. 'Fern was in really bad pain!' he recalled.

By now she was in floods of tears and Phil knew that he had to get her to hospital as soon as possible. Grabbing hold of her arm, he tried to lift her to her feet. But she refused to budge an inch.

'Please, Fern,' he begged. 'I know it's hard, but you need to stand up.'

'I can't,' she mumbled. 'Just leave me a minute. It hurts too much.' But as far as Phil was concerned, they had little time to spare. For all he knew, both Fern and their unborn baby could be in grave danger. The sooner she was in a hospital ward, the better.

Growing desperate, he tried to lift Fern. He had little success. She felt like a dead weight. Her limbs were hanging limply from her side. Phil could feel his cheeks burning and his stomach was starting to turn. He was rapidly beginning to panic. 'Please!' he screamed, now at his wits' end.

Realising that she had little choice, Fern braced herself and started to move. Getting down the stairs proved particularly tricky. Using one arm to steady himself on the banister, Phil wrapped the other round Fern's waist and helped to lift her down, one step at a time. For the first time ever in his life (and hopefully the last), he wished that they had had a stair lift installed!

'It took us forty minutes to get from the bedroom down to the car,' he said, exhausted even by the memory. 'She was crying her eyes out. I said, "Come on, we've got to go to the hospital." I was starting to lose my temper! Then she sobs: "I can't, I haven't taken my make-up off!"'

It may have seemed like a ridiculous request to Phil, but Fern defended her outburst. The night before they had been out to dinner with friends and Fern had been feeling particularly pasty and had applied an extra layer of make-up just to look half human! It had been an enjoyable evening, but by 10.00 pm Fern was begging to go home and straight to bed. Once inside the house, she could barely speak. She even skipped her pre-bedtime cup of herbal tea. Instead, she dragged herself into bed and crashed out almost instantly. She barely had time to take her shoes off, let alone her make-up. She knew she would regret it in the morning, but right then she could not care less. Phil did not have the heart to wake her. She had been in an awful amount of pain that week and dearly needed a good rest.

'Well, when you go to bed with your make-up on you feel awful in the morning,' explained Fern. 'Also, I hadn't cleaned my teeth but he wouldn't let me do that either! We staggered into the maternity unit and he blithely tells them all: "Do you know, she wanted to take her make-up off!" And all the midwifes were like, "Yes, what's wrong with that?"'

Dripping with sweat, his face wrought with anxiety, Phil was stunned by their blasé response. Fern, however, started giggling. 'Women understand!' she protested. At least something had brought a smile to her face, he thought with a sigh.

Fern was taken straight to a special ward and given drugs to relieve her pain. Sitting by her bedside with a paper coffee cup in his hand, Phil was reluctant to leave Fern for even a minute. By nightfall, the nurses advised him to return home and get some sleep. The baby would not be arriving any time soon and the hospital was short of beds as it was! After some persuasion, Phil returned home.

Under Fern's instruction, he returned the next day with an overnight bag. He had hardly slept a wink that night and was desperate to return to the hospital. Luckily, Fern's mother, Ruth, had been on stand-by to look after the kids. After splashing his face with cold water and wolfing down a bowl of cornflakes, he jumped into the car and sped down to the hospital.

Phil proudly presented Fern with her washbag. In all honesty, he could barely recall what he had actually packed. He had been in such a daze that morning and had simply grabbed a handful of clothes from Fern's lingerie drawer and a few items from the bathroom cabinet. Pulling each item out one by one, Fern looked utterly confused. 'He arrived with a bag containing a couple of shirts – no bottoms, a tiny bar towel and no bottoms!' Phil looked shamefully at the pile of useless items on Fern's bed. He had been given one simple task to complete and he could not even manage that! What sort of parent would he make? Fortunately, Fern saw the funny side and reassured him that there was nothing to worry about. At least her top half would look presentable. She would be spending most of her time in bed anyway.

However, Fern soon realised that she would need more than a few tops when doctors informed her that she was in for longer than an overnight stay. There had been some further complications with her fibroid and she would need to remain under close observation. 'I was laid up in hospital for about a fortnight,' said Fern. 'My fibroid made everything in the pregnancy a lot more complicated.'

Officially, the baby was not due for another four weeks or so, but doctors discovered that they would have to act quickly if mother and child were to have a safe birth. Fern's pain was growing stronger by the day and there was a limit to how much she could tolerate.

'The problem was that because I had had so many painkilling injections they realised that they would have to deliver her, even though that would mean she would arrive four weeks early,' said Fern.

Looking back, Fern is extremely grateful to the fantastic medical team that she had around her. She recalled the moment when her doctor first broke the news. Sitting down beside her, he lowered his clipboard and placed his glasses on her bedside table. 'Of course, the decision is completely yours,' he told Fern. 'You could wait a little longer, but there is a limit to the dosage of drugs we can administer. At the same time, you can expect to endure even more pain than you have to date. I'm not going to lie to you. It won't be easy.'

With the doctor's help, Fern and Phil weighed up the pros and cons. The decision seemed obvious. Fern could barely sustain this pain for another day, let alone four more weeks: 'I had a brilliant doctor and he gave me the choice of staying in pain and in hospital and waiting it out or stopping the pain and having her delivered.'

Holed up in hospital, Fern had little idea of what was going on in the outside world. The producers on *This Morning* were having a terrible time. Richard and Judy's departure in 2001 had left them in a state of flux. Letters of complaint were arriving at the offices on a daily basis, as regular viewers protested fiercely about the new format. They complained that the new team was 'wooden and stilted'. Within four weeks, style icon Twiggy was on her way out with a pay-off and a bruised ego.

The producers had to act quickly if they were to save the show. Everyone was agreed – Fern Britton was their only hope. They were fully aware of her reluctance to return to work, but she was the perfect candidate. It was her mum-next-door quality that pulled in the viewers. No one else even came close. Over the summer, Granada had screen-tested dozens of actresses, including the likes of former *Coronation Street* star Denise Welch. Crossing their fingers, they contacted her agent, Jon, with an offer of work.

'When we first talked about it, I was literally in hospital giving birth!' said Fern. 'Phil kept coming in with messages from Jon explaining what was happening.'

Whereas in the past she had been steadfastly against the

idea, now Fern was starting to consider it as a viable option. At the time, Phil was still working on the show as one of the programme's chefs. If she were to take the full-time position, she would at least have Phil by her side. Working together on *Ready Steady Cook* had been great fun and was something that she had always intended to do again. Phil would usually come into the hospital with tales of on-set antics and Fern had to admit that she did miss the camaraderie of working with a regular team.

'I have missed it more than I thought I was going to,' she confessed. 'I suppose it's because Phil has still been working there and tells me everything that has been going on.'

'They're really desperate to have you back,' enthused her agent, Jon. 'They'll do almost anything to secure your services. The public support has been incredible!'

Fern was both shocked and flattered by his words. 'I would be lying if I didn't say that I was extremely flattered to be asked back,' she admitted. 'And asked to come back a bit quicker than I thought I was going to be.'

But she still had her reservations. With a newborn baby due in a matter of days, a career move was the last thing she should have been considering. Phil and Fern discussed the matter at great length, and Phil could see that deep down Fern wanted to take on the job – she had never been able to resist a challenge. There was no denying that she was a great mother and wife, but her talents were almost wasted in the home. Selfishly, Phil would have loved Fern all for himself, but she had a commitment to her fans. There was no reason why he could not share her with the rest of the world.

Fern was extremely confused and flustered. Something was urging her to accept the job, but, logistically, how would it work? How would she do the school run, breast-feed her new baby and step into Judy Finnegan's shoes all at the same time? Surely she would have a nervous breakdown. Phil could see that her thoughts were spiralling out of control. He recognised his cue to step in and help her make a decision.

'Phil just put his arms around me and said that I had to go for it,' said Fern. 'He knew I wanted to do it, but I just didn't see how I could cope with everything.'

Thankfully, Phil had other ideas. 'He had it all worked out,' continued Fern. 'He said he would give me total support, even putting part of his work on the back-burner for a while if need be.' Fern was incredibly touched; no one had ever been prepared to make that sort of sacrifice for her before. Overcome by emotion, she started to cry. 'I burst into tears,' she said. 'I knew there were men in this world who would make such a sacrifice, but I never thought I would end up with one.'

Amid those tears, something in Fern's mind changed. For the first time, the impossible seemed possible. With Phil behind her, she could achieve anything: 'At that moment, I started to realise that, yes, this could be done.'

Acting as Fern's go-between, Phil relayed the information to her agent, Jon, who in turn passed on the good news to the *This Morning* team. Predictably, they were overjoyed and within days they came back with a rather substantial offer. But Fern had little time to celebrate or even register what was happening; she had more important things on her mind!

'I was in hospital, literally having the baby, when Phil came in and said he had my agent on the phone and that I had got the job,' said Fern. 'It wasn't the first thing on my mind at the time as you can imagine!'

Just as with her previous children, Fern was told by doctors that she would have to give birth by caesarean section. Unlike many celebrities 'too posh to push', Fern would rather have given birth naturally, but she had little choice. Because of her painful fibroid, it would have been too dangerous. 'I had her by caesarean because that's how I'd had the other children and they said there was no option.'

Phil rushed to Fern's side. Taking hold of her hand tightly, he refused to let go even for a second. Offering soothing words, he made Fern feel completely at ease. In that instant, she felt for all those single mothers in the world forced to give birth without a partner by her side, and she felt extremely privileged to have a man as loving and as understanding as Phil. 'He held my hand throughout the whole thing,' she smiled.

Even the staff were impressed by Phil's attentiveness. He remained admirably calm throughout the whole birth and was not at all squeamish. 'I've never seen such an excited father in all my years!' exclaimed one consultant. When Fern finally gave birth, Phil could hardly contain himself. His eyes glazed over as Fern cradled their newborn baby girl. Phil remarked on how delicate and fragile she looked. He was almost afraid to pick her up for fear of crushing her.

Both parents had already agreed on the name Winifred Theresa Violet. Rather than being names picked randomly from a book, each had some significance. 'My grandmother was called Winifred and we chose the name Violet because all the girls in my family have to have a flower name or a shrub,' explained Fern. 'There's a Cherry, Rose and a Jasmine. Gracie's middle name is Bluebell.' Though Fern had first suggested the name Winifred, it had instantly struck a chord with Phil: 'My mother had a great-auntie Winnie and Theresa is my mum's name.'

Fern and Phil both preferred the abbreviation Winnie. After all, it was far better suited to a baby. 'But once she's a funky teenager, she'll probably be called Fred!' laughed Fern.

It was a wonderfully poignant moment. Dazed and confused, Fern had almost forgotten herself. Her 'Fern Britton' pill had well and truly worn off. No longer everyone's favourite television presenter, she was simply Fern, mother of a beautiful new baby. It had been a wonderful birth – if only because Phil had accompanied her on the journey from beginning to end. But there had also been several comedic moments!

'Winnie had just been delivered, everyone's rushing around her and I'm watching this nurse check her over,' said Fern, giggling at the memory. 'Then the anaesthetist turns to me and says: "When can I get on *Ready Steady Cook* then?" He's coming on in November!'

To everyone's relief, both mother and daughter were in good health. Fern was exhausted, but glad that the pain from her fibroid had finally subsided. 'That particular pain went,' she says. 'Then it was post-operative pain, but they look after you terribly well.'

Her thoughts then turned to Grace, Jack and Harry. Her mother, Ruth, had taken them on holiday to give Fern and Phil some peace and quiet, and Fern was grateful for the space, but she missed them desperately. The plan had been to bring them back in time for the birth, but because Winnie arrived so unexpectedly, that was not possible. She could not wait to introduce their new little sister to them. 'Because she came so early, they were on holiday in Cornwall,' lamented Fern. 'On the one hand, it was lovely because it was just Phil and I, but I wanted them to be there.'

Phil phoned Ruth to break the news. A week later, they returned from holiday. By now, Fern was out of hospital and resting at home. Jack and Harry were laden with gifts for their new little sister; they had helped pick out teddy bears and newborn baby toys. On seeing Winnie for the first time, they were fascinated by her size. She looked almost like a toy herself! Grace was particularly enamoured by what appeared to be a replica of her own baby doll. Although they were not allowed to hold her, they could not wait to touch her little fingers and toes. 'They came home with presents and toys,' smiled Fern. 'They were jumping about and fighting over who was having their picture taken with her.'

Smiling to herself, Fern felt incredibly lucky. Watching her three kids run rings round Phil as he cradled Winnie in his arms, she thought to herself, 'I must be the luckiest woman alive.'

Chapter 10

Rising to the Challenge
– The Working Mum

With three children already under her wing, Fern could rightfully consider herself an old hand at bringing up babies. In marked comparison, Phil was stepping into totally new territory. But Fern enjoyed teaching him about parenthood, as it made her own experience even more pleasurable.

Fern had warned Phil that he would not be getting any beauty sleep for the next few weeks! Like all newborns, Winnie could not make it through the night without waking up crying. At first, Phil struggled to get out of bed, but he was determined not to let Fern do all the hard work. Bleary-eyed, he would prise himself from beneath the covers and run to Winnie's aid. After a while, Phil settled into a rhythm and it did not seem half as hard as he had imagined.

Friends would remark enviously on how relaxed Fern and Phil appeared to be; nothing fazed them. 'She's not sleeping at night but I don't feel exhausted,' shrugged Fern. 'I think I've paced myself better this time. It's much easier to cope when it's your fourth child. I'm not quite as hysterical about everything as I was during my previous pregnancies.'

Everyone agreed that Fern was a far more relaxed mother this time around. 'With my first three, I was an anxious mum, fussing around and convincing myself I was making a mess of everything,' she admitted. 'With Winnie, I'm much more relaxed, partly because of experience, partly because I'm a happier person now.'

For the most part, Winnie was a peaceful child and gave her parents few problems. 'She's very happy and contented,' declared Fern proudly. Phil also did everything in his power to make sure that Fern felt at ease. She had carried his child for months and had endured intense physical pain. The least he could do was to bring her a cup of tea every morning! 'Phil brings me tea every morning, which is like having a diamond necklace every day.' Fern told her friends proudly.

He also stepped up his responsibilities to Grace and the twins. Whereas Fern had always prepared their breakfasts and packed lunches, now Phil took on this duty. Fern would joke to her kids that they must be the envy of the playground. Not everyone had a gourmet chef preparing their lunchbox: 'He feeds the children and takes it in turns to take the kids to school. He's a top dad and a top stepdad. He doesn't put a foot wrong! Instinctively he knows what Winnie needs and what to do. He will even get up in the middle of the night and sort her out.'

Phil was more than happy to help out. There was nothing heroic about his actions; he just wished he could do more: 'Women just take it all on board, getting up in the night, feeding. They never whinge, never moan. There's not a lot I can do other than say, "Are you all right, love? Because I can't breast-feed."'

From the outset Phil had told Fern that he wanted an equal share of parenting responsibilities. Biologically, it went without saying that there were certain tasks only a mother could perform, but wherever possible, Phil was eager to help out. The couple even purchased a baby sling so that Phil could carry Winnie about. 'She is so tiny that she doesn't really fit it at the moment,' he smiled. But whenever Phil did take Winnie out in public, he was bombarded with female attention. He joked to his single male friends that they might want to borrow Winnie for the afternoon! 'I must say I have never been chatted up by so many octogenarian women as when I'm with the baby!' he exclaimed.

One thing Phil had not been prepared for was the amount of attention a baby required. He soon discovered that it was impossible to do anything. Unable to let her out of his sight for even a second, he found himself stumbling round the house with a baby permanently glued to his hip. 'You can't do anything!' he sighed. 'You can't go to the loo, you can't eat or read a paper. I've worked out how to eat holding a baby in one arm.'

One night, Phil agreed to take care of Winnie for the evening while Fern went to visit some friends. She had had a tough few months and deserved some time off. Unfortunately, Phil later realised that the England football team was playing an important game that day, which was being broadcast live on television. He deliberated about what to do. There was no way he could miss the game, so he concluded that as long as he kept the volume to a minimum everything would be fine. Cradling Winnie in his arms, he settled on the sofa and flicked on the television. As the game progressed, however, he became more and more animated. As David Beckham weaved his way into the penalty box, Phil momentarily forgot himself and screamed loudly! Suddenly, he felt a movement in his arms. 'I was holding her watching the England game the other night,' he told a friend. 'She jumped when I started shouting!'

One of Fern's greatest fears was that her children would be jealous of a new arrival in her household. She was also very sensitive to the possibility that, as Phil's biological daughter, Winnie might receive preferential treatment, but Phil assured her that that would never be the case. He loved all four children dearly and equally and that would never change. To Fern's relief, her other kids took to Winnie quite quickly. 'There's a little bit of "Mummy's attention is taken away" but they all really adore her,' assured Fern. 'I find one of them saying "I love you so much" to her every day.'

Although Fern had overcome the problem of her painful fibroid, one other complication surrounded Winnie's birth. Fern feared that the debilitating postnatal depression that had plagued her previous pregnancies would return. After Grace was born, one doctor had suggested that Fern's diet could be partly to blame. Wishing to take every precaution possible, she made an appointment to see a nutritionist. 'When I knew I was pregnant this time, I saw a nutritionist to get my diet straightened out,' she explained. 'Then, about a month before Winnie was born, she gave me zinc and vitamin B_6 drops to take.' Phil also helped Fern formulate a meal plan that was rich in essential vitamins and minerals. She found herself eating foods that she would never have imagined eating before and actually felt better than she had done in years! All the hard work had definitely paid off. 'There hasn't been a glint of depression this time!' she announced proudly.

But Fern secretly still lived in the fear that her depression would return. Giving birth to Winnie brought back terrible memories of the ordeal she had been through. 'When you're suffering from postnatal depression you think you're not coping,' she deduced. 'You pretend to everyone you're fine, but inside you're completely bleak. You're not able to get out of bed, aren't looking forward to anything, don't want to see anybody.

'When you've been through postnatal depression, you are very aware of the possibility of it coming back. I was determined that if I did get it after having Winnie, it would be recognised quickly and treated.'

Understanding the situation and sympathising with her completely, Phil was on hand to pick up the pieces should Fern ever fall apart. Thankfully, she never did. Doctors and nurses rallied round to make sure that she had the best medical care possible. 'So far so good!' Fern told one magazine. 'I've been very well looked after by my GP who is ready to spot any symptoms.'

With a safety net securely in place, Fern felt totally reassured. Even if her age-old problems did resurface, this time she would not be coping alone.

'The minute Winnie was born, they were looking out for me,' she says appreciatively. Her doctors also suggested that she should start weekly sessions with a psychiatrist. 'Phil and I would go together and he would say how he thought I was doing, and I would say how I thought I was doing,' she said.

At first, Fern felt apprehensive about attending the sessions, but she was willing to give anything a try. She did have visions of reclining on a *chaise longue* while a gentleman in a white coat asked questions about her childhood. Phil even joked that they would be carrying her out in a strait-jacket! But thankfully those preconceptions were a million miles from the reality.

'It wasn't therapy,' Fern pointed out. 'Just someone

looking out for me. She wasn't a psychiatrist in a white coat. It was just like a friend chatting to a friend. It was very nice to have somebody listen to me prattling on for an hour once a week.'

They would discuss everything, from inconsequential remarks to significant incidents. Nothing was too trivial. Of course, Fern could always lean on Phil, but it was pleasing to know that she would not always have to burden him. Sometimes it helped to speak with someone completely removed from the situation, and Fern was highly impressed with the results. 'After about six weeks, she said, "You're absolutely fine,"' beamed Fern.

Despite her celebrity status, Fern also opted to seek treatment through the NHS. She never once expected to be fast-tracked or treated any differently because of her fame. 'I did it all on the NHS!' she said proudly. 'All my babies were born on the NHS and I received the most wonderful care.'

Feeling far more emotionally secure, Fern felt comfortable sharing her experiences with the rest of the world. In a bid to wipe out any stigma attached to depression, she agreed to speak openly about her battle. She presented a *Tonight With Trevor McDonald* programme on the subject and was appointed patron of the charity Perinatal Illness UK (PNI-UK). Making the documentary brought back memories of her own depression, but Fern felt that she had a responsibility to help others suffering a similar fate. 'If there are any women in that position, go to your doctor for help. I want people to know you're not alone,' she said.

Most importantly of all, Fern wished to highlight that postnatal depression could happen to anyone. Dealing with a newborn baby was tough. Pregnancy itself was a hormonal rollercoaster, leaving most new mothers emotionally distraught, but an inability to cope did not denote failure. Rather than suffer in silence, Fern urged new mothers to seek help. It was something she wished she'd done a long time ago!

'There isn't anybody in the world with an ordinary, simple, easy life,' sighed Fern. 'It's nonsense to think, "Well, it's all right for you." Everybody has troubles. But you can get round it. I've had times in my life when I never thought I'd ever, ever feel happiness again. I was very good at pretending I was happy. I was very good at smiling, but I was bloody miserable. I was suicidal!'

Along with expert medical help, Fern credited much of her recovery to Phil. Her life had completely changed the day they started dating, and he had supported her through some of the toughest times of her life. By all accounts, she felt like a new person and it was mostly down to him.

'Depression has been with me for a long, long time,' she confessed. 'Ever since I was young, I've had very difficult times but I'm so glad that something kept me going because now I feel constantly happy. Phil's seen me through great depths of despair and he's never wavered once. He's a very special man.'

'When I had the boys I felt like shit all the time and when I had Grace my marriage was falling apart, so that didn't help. So it is blissful, now, to have a child and really enjoy it,' she said. 'I feel fitter and better than I have done for years. And I'm sure the fact that I'm so happy has a huge amount to do with that. That's because of Phil. He is a very supportive, true partner.'

Winnie's birth had come as something of a miracle to Phil and Fern. Given Fern's age and medical conditions, the couple knew they were extremely lucky. But any thoughts of extending the family further were now out of the question. Phil had watched Fern endure excruciating pain and he could never put her through that again. 'After Grace, the gynaecologist looked at the fibroid and said, "Oh, that's a leave-well-alone job,"' said Fern. 'But after Winnie, she saw it and said it had calcified – turned into stone, like pumice. She decided to leave it because if you cut fibroids out you can cause a haemorrhage. If it causes me problems at a later date, I'd have to have a hysterectomy at the click of a finger. So having more children isn't a very good idea.'

For the time being, Fern chose to put off a hysterectomy for as long as possible. She had been through enough physical traumas. As long as she was not planning to have any more children in the near future, her doctor advised her that the operation was not urgent. 'One day I will have to get it sorted out if it makes things difficult for me. But while it's not giving me any hassle, I believe in leaving well alone,' Fern said.

Both Phil and Fern agreed it was unlikely they would extend the family. With four kids running riot, they already had enough on their plate. 'I don't think so,' grinned Phil, shaking his head. 'I think this is it.'

Nodding her head fiercely, Fern agreed. 'If some miracle happened, it would be fantastic. But I think I'm rather too old. I've had four by the age of forty-four so I don't think I'll be having five by the age of forty-five!'

Besides, it was not worth the physical risk. 'I'd have to book my hospital bed from day one!' she joked. But there was a serious side to her situation: 'I don't think I could go through that ordeal again. I said to Phil that I thought it might actually kill me if I did.'

Fern had been extremely lucky so far. She knew it was wise to quit while she was ahead. There were thousands of couples in the world unable to have children and Fern was lucky enough to four! She should simply sit back and appreciate the gifts she had been given. 'You can only take your luck and blessings so far,' she reasoned. 'You have four healthy children and you can't ask for any more than that. Anyway, once you get past two, you don't notice!'

With her newborn baby and a new job on the horizon, Fern had more than enough to keep herself busy. The bosses at Granada were extremely keen for Fern to start work as soon as she was ready. They understood her position and were willing to bend over backwards to accommodate her every need. About six weeks after the birth, Fern met up with bosses to discuss a plan of action.

Ironically, it was Fern who suggested returning to work earlier than had first been contemplated. 'The opportunity arrived far more quickly than I expected,' she explained. 'But I was itching to get back.'

'It was me who suggested going back as of 5 November for three days a week and then four days a week in the New Year,' she said proudly. So, just twelve weeks after lying in a hospital bed, Fern would be back in the presenting hot seat. It was quite a tall order, but Fern took the challenge firmly in her stride. She felt ready: 'It gave me six weeks of being at home with Winnie and getting my head around the idea of going back to work early.'

On the outside, Fern was a picture of confidence, but inside she secretly had her reservations. In moments of panic, she would turn to Phil and ask if she were doing the right thing. Was she being selfish and neglecting her duties as a mother? He always managed to calm her down with words of warmth and encouragement.

'I have no idea how I will manage!' she admitted. 'But I am determined that Winnie won't miss out just because I want to go back to work.'

In the past, Fern had employed a full-time nanny to help out with the kids, but she adamantly refused to go down that road again. As a single mother, it had been impossible to bring up children and have a career, but with Phil now by her side there was no excuse. Her children deserved as much of her time as possible. 'I'm not going to have a full-time nanny this time round,' she promised. 'A lovely neighbour who is a child minder is going to help out.'

By the time Fern returned to work, she had a successful system in place. 'My mum helps me out two days a week and a wonderful lady called Sue helps me two days a week. They have done since my twin boys were born seven years ago.'

Phil was also eager to assist wherever possible. Back at the hospital, he had promised Fern that he would support her 100 per cent. No matter what, he would remain true to his word and he was an extremely loyal man. 'Phil is going to take on a lot of the household responsibilities,' said Fern.

Now that he no longer worked at the hotel, Phil could be a lot more flexible with his time. The first few weeks worked out perfectly. 'Because I'm self-employed, I work a lot from home,' he explained. 'The television stuff fitted in quite nicely as all the programmes were on a summer break. I've just started back on *This Morning*.'

Although Fern knew she could pull it off, she still had her reservations about performing such a juggling act. 'There is still a battle going on in my mind about children versus work,' she complained. 'I'm not fiercely ambitious and work is not the be-all and end-all of my life. I'm far more likely to camp outside the sales than I am outside a television studio asking for a job!'

'When I was younger I always intended to work for a bit, get married, have a family and then not work much and enjoy being a mum,' she continued. But I've ended up working as well as having children and I never thought I'd be that sort of person. I'm thrilled and delighted that I have a wonderful job, for which I get paid very well, but it's certainly not the most important thing in the world.'

'I have never been particularly ambitious and I'm certainly not prepared to put my career before my children. To be honest, I could be a full-time mother no problem. I can imagine myself staying at home all day, yes. I can also see myself working somewhere like Marks & Spencer. I don't know who said you had to be ambitious to get ahead in television. I sometimes wonder if I have an ambitious bone in my body!'

Her main concern was that the children would suffer. She promised herself that if any of her kids felt at all neglected, she would give up her work in an instant. 'The bottom line is that if I missed a single school sports day because of work, I would be beside myself with guilt. But I never have.'

Any concerns she might have had were soon dispelled. Phil convinced her that she was doing a great job. Pangs of mother's guilt were natural, but no one could ever accuse her of being a bad mother! 'I don't know how we have made it work but we have!' she would later declare with relief. 'All I would say to people who worry about when's the best time to have a baby, is just to get on with it. It does work itself out.'

As it turned out, Fern had been worrying about nothing. Her kids were perfectly happy and never once wanted for Fern's attentions. 'I haven't missed out on anything in my children's lives,' said Fern proudly. She made the realisation one morning, when taking the twins to school. Phil was working and it was her turn to drop them off. She was still clearing away the remainder of the breakfast debris when she heard the boys calling from the front door. 'Come on, Mummy, we're going to be late!' they complained. Fern was stunned to see them ready and waiting. There was a time when she would literally have to drag them out of bed!

On the way to school, Jack and Harry chatted animatedly about their lessons for the day. 'Surely this wasn't right,' Fern thought to herself. 'Weren't kids supposed to loathe school?' But as Fern kissed her sons goodbye, something almost miraculous happened. 'Mummy, I really love school!' chirped Harry, as she went to kiss him.

'How fantastic is that?' cooed Fern. 'I'd know I'd failed as a mother if the children were screaming, "Mummy, don't go to work." If that happened, I would give up the job. Somebody once said to me that you can't live your life for your children, but I would quite happily do that and I don't think I'd miss out on anything. I adore work, but if push came to shove I would stay at home.'

Fortunately, the producers on *This Morning* had been extremely sensitive to Fern's needs. They agreed that Winnie could accompany Fern to the studio. 'I'm very privileged!' admitted Fern. 'I used to take Gracie with me until she was about a year old.' Fern recalled how she would sneak off to see her daughter in between breaks. One minute she would be in front of the cameras, the next she would be nuzzling her child to her chest. She imagined a similar scenario with Winnie.

'To begin with, Winnie will come in with me to the studio because I'm still breast-feeding her,' she explained. 'I've just had her travel cot delivered to be set up in my dressing room. At the moment she is sleeping from 10.00 am until noon, which is perfect timing because that's when I'll be on air. A couple of women at work have said they will look after her and Phil is there on Mondays so, of course, he will help out.'

She continued 'I don't think it's going to scar Winnie for life and, I must say, I'm quite looking forward to having two hours of not having to think about her because I will know that she is in safe hands. All I want to do is to concentrate on the show for two hours and then race back to my dressing room to be with her the minute I finish.'

Fern's main worry had been that she might take on too much and fall into a deep depression, but she appeared to have everything under control: 'My biggest concern is becoming ill again juggling family life and work. I must pace myself. Luckily, I've got my head around things now.'

But juggling work and family life was not the only challenge facing Fern. She also had the enormous task of raising ratings for *This Morning*. Since Richard and Judy's departure, viewing figures for the show had fallen off massively. Fern had been drafted in to save the show and expectations were high. With the show's future riding on her shoulders, it was a wonder that Fern did not collapse under the pressure. She was under no illusion that it would be an easy task. Both Fern and the production team were agreed that they had their work cut out! They had been through figures and discussed the matter at great length, but, unperturbed, she was optimistic about the future: 'The ratings have levelled out at around one million. In previous years, they have averaged about 1.4 million so we have lost 400,000 viewers. The goal is to get the figure back up to 1.4 million and if we can achieve it that would be fantastic. I'm not saying I'm the sole person to do it, but as part of the team I hope we can.'

Fern had already worked with John Leslie one day a week on the show and the pair had a great rapport. 'John Leslie and I already work well together,' she said confidently. 'And I'm looking forward to working with Colleen Nolan. I feel rather bad that, for the past few weeks, John and Colleen have been at the coalface taking loads of flak while I've been sitting on my arse at home having a nice time. So I think it's about time I went in and did my bit.'

Fern was confident that, at its core, *This Morning* was still a popular show. In fact, it was a national institution! She had always been a fan and would have hated to see it disappear for good. But she had a good feeling about the next few months. She would do everything in her power to save this sinking ship.

'I do feel that we can win viewers back so all we can do is give it a whirl,' she shrugged. '*This Morning* is a programme that is very well known and loved and, if we can't make it work, then we are obviously the wrong people.'

Secretly, Fern relished the challenge. Even though she loved being at home, she was looking forward to getting her teeth back into work. 'I love being at home with my family but this time I'm really looking forward to going back to work,' she enthused. 'I think it's because I haven't been pressured to go back. After every baby, I think I'm never going to work again, then all of a sudden some wonderful big job turns up.'

Working with the *This Morning* team was like a dream come true and Fern soon came to consider them as an extended family. And Fern need not have worried about Winnie not getting enough attention – she had people running round after her constantly! Unlike most of the working population, Fern particularly loved Mondays. It was the day that Phil worked with her in the studio. She loved the fact that she, Phil and Winnie could spend time together between filming and she knew that she was in an extremely privileged position!

'This is the only show I have ever wanted to do!' she gushed. 'I was built for it, and to be given the opportunity to present it is unbelievable. It is the most enjoyable job I have ever had!' But unlike Richard and Judy, Fern did not see herself presenting the show for a further thirteen years!

'I don't know how they did it!' she exclaimed. Our line of work has a shelf-life and you never know how long that is. What I do know is that I will be there until 12 July 2003, and if they don't want me after that I'll be quite happy to stack shelves in a supermarket!'

As it turned out, the producers would extend Fern's contract far beyond 2003. As viewers warmed to her friendly, down-to earth manner, the ratings soared, and Fern Britton was hailed as the saviour of daytime television.

Chapter 11

Christmases and Controversy

From Granada bosses to public viewers, everyone thanked their lucky stars that Fern had agreed on a premature return to work. It appeared she had managed to do the impossible and save an ailing television show while also caring for a newborn baby. As usual, Fern made hard work look like a breeze, but the reality was very different.

From the very beginning, Fern knew she had a difficult task ahead. 'It does take a lot to get me out of the house!' she said in jest. 'But I do love *This Morning* and that's the only reason I did it. It was very difficult because Winnie was still so small. For the first year I was up four or five times a night, and it wasn't good. In the end, if I got two hours' sleep in a row, I was doing well!'

Bleary-eyed, Fern would stagger out of bed and cradle Winnie in her arms. On plenty of occasions, Phil would go in her place, but as she was breast-feeding, inevitably, Fern had to get up, too. Consequently, she would arrive at work looking exhausted. As time wore on, she spent longer in make-up, applying layers of concealer to hide her bags and she frequently praised the make-up girls on *This Morning* for doing such a fantastic job! 'I'm not susceptible to many things, but when I'm tired my right eye waters,' she confessed. 'So all of my make-up is waterproof. If I'm really tired, both eyes water!'

Fern was also reluctant to let Winnie out of her sight: 'Winnie came everywhere with me, and I used to leave the set in the news breaks to go and feed her. It was exhausting – getting her up and dressed, getting her in the car seat and getting to work.' It takes most mothers a good hour to get a newborn baby out of the house. Often, Fern had just thirty minutes. 'Then straight after work, I'd give her some lunch, get back in the car and go and pick up the other children from school on the way home.'

By the time Fern reached her front door, she was frazzled. Luckily, Phil would always have a cup of tea brewed and something tasty in the oven. Fern would rest her tired legs and Phil would give her a relaxing foot massage. Fern often joked that he had missed his vocation. It must be down to kneading all that pastry dough, he claimed.

'I never intended to be the kind of mother who gave

birth and was back at work two hours later,' insisted Fern. 'But life has a strange way of turning out. Every time I had a baby I was offered a better job straight away. It was difficult and I talk to the children a lot about how much I am there and not there.'

Now old enough to understand, the twins loved to watch their mother on television. Everyone at school would rush round them asking if Fern Britton really was their mummy. But it was the other mothers (not to mention the fathers) who were worse! They would hang around the school gates, waiting to catch a glimpse of Fern. Some were even bold enough to ask for her autograph. Even when she had only had two hours' sleep the night before, she was always happy to oblige.

'The boys are getting to the stage where they are very proud of me now,' smiled Fern. 'When I was doing *Ready Steady Cook*, they never wanted to watch because they thought it was boring. But now they quite like the kudos of having a mum on television, I think.'

In some ways, Fern did regret returning to work so soon after the birth; she would have preferred to spend a few more weeks at home with Winnie. But she had little option: 'There's a likelihood the show wouldn't still be around had we not all pulled together. I'm very proud we rescued it.'

Besides, there were a quite a few advantages! Working with Phil was fantastic. 'That's the best thing about working on TV together,' said Phil. 'I can pop in on

Winnie when I'm off-air and I get to pinch Fern's bum when she's in the kitchen!'

'It's true!' laughed Fern. 'And just before we're about to go on air, Phil walks past where John Leslie and I sit and if I'm wearing anything at all revealing, he'll give me a cheeky wink. No one else notices, but I know what he's thinking!'

Additionally, there were financial advantages to taking on the job – Fern was offered an extremely lucrative deal to return to *This Morning* full time. When the show was later recommissioned, she became the highest-paid woman on television with an estimated £500,000 deal for a three-day week, and the news made national headlines. Fern denied the figure, saying it had been blown out of all proportion, but did admit that she had been offered a great deal of money. 'I can't possibly justify it,' she said shaking her head, 'when you look at what nurses are paid.'

Admittedly, Fern felt guilty for commanding such a high salary, but she reassured herself that it was going towards a good cause. By now, Fern's family had outgrown their house. With Winnie's arrival, they decided that it was definitely time to look for a new home. 'We've had to buy a new house now there are six of us,' said Fern. 'We were getting a bit short of space, especially as we've got all Phil's cookery equipment and his motorbikes there.'

After much searching, the couple found a dream property in High Wycombe. It needed a lot of renovating, but Fern and Phil saw it as another challenging project. 'The new house needs some work, so we won't be moving in for a while,' said Fern. All the money I earn from *This Morning* over this year is going into the house, so by this time next year we'll be skint but very happy.'

Aside from the usual teething problems of caring for a newborn baby, life in Fern's household was extremely happy. Even though she and Phil were working like dogs during the day and up half the night caring for Winnie, they rarely lost their temper with each other.

'I have never been as happy as I am now,' insisted Fern. 'Phil really is the most wonderful man. Sometimes we can lie in bed at 3.00 am if the baby has just woken us up and we'll be laughing helplessly about something stupid. It is a proper friendship and partnership, apart from the fact that I fancy the pants off him. I wasn't quite sure what women meant when they said, "My husband is my best friend," but now I do and it's lovely.'

While Fern and Phil were madly in love, Fern had to admit that she still felt a shadow of insecurity. The failure of her last marriage had left her feeling emotionally vulnerable and at the time she had sworn never to place her trust in another man. But then Phil came along and changed everything. She trusted him more than anyone before in her life. But allowing herself to fall in love had been a struggle; it was difficult to let go of all those hang-ups. Even though she knew it would never happen, she dreaded waking up one morning to discover an empty pillow beside her.

'I know that if Phil did leave me, I'd cope,' she sighed.

'I have done before.' But it was not a situation she liked to imagine. 'Luckily, he feels that little bit of insecurity too,' she continued.

One night, while lying in bed, Fern admitted her fears to Phil. Looking into her eyes, he promised that would never happen. No one even compared to Fern. He was more worried another man might come and sweep her away. She had so many admirers! So they made a pact: 'He said that he wouldn't run off with someone younger if I would promise not to either,' said Fern.

As Christmas 2001 approached, Fern and Phil's sense of family strengthened even further. The couple were especially excited about this year's festive season as Winnie would be celebrating Christmas for the very first time. Determined to make it a special occasion, they agreed to pull out all the stops. 'This will be our first family Christmas with Winnie and we can't wait!' said Phil. They drew up a list of potential guests, consisting of family and friends. They ruthlessly tried to keep numbers down but still came up with a figure of twenty-two.

Fern and Phil agreed to split the preparation duties. After Fern's mince-pie disaster the previous year, she decided to steer well clear of the kitchen. Her forte was gift buying and decorating. 'Fern and I have an agreement,' explained Phil. 'She lays the table and buys the presents. I normally cook for 200 so twenty-two is nothing.'

But whenever Phil needed a break, Fern was always ready

to rush into the kitchen and keep an eye on proceedings. 'I do get sick of cooking sometimes,' he confessed.

Fern took great pride in decorating the house and made her preparations weeks beforehand. 'For me, it's all about the tinsel, baubles and candles that make it Christmas,' she exclaimed excitedly. 'I'm worse than the kids! I buy the tree early, then I dig out all the old decorations and the little papier-mâché nativity sets that the kids have made. I treasure them all.'

Phil spent weeks testing out recipes and conjuring up interesting variations on classic dishes. In order to minimise the stress, he decided to keep the meal simple. Besides, with so many children at the table he did not want to over-complicate dishes with fancy ingredients that were too rich for their palette. He had always maintained that Christmas dinner was one of those meals where tradition prevailed over innovation.

'My advice is to keep the meal very simple,' he told friends. 'Do all your preparation on Christmas Eve so you don't get stressed. I buy things like cranberry sauce because I know I will never be able to make it as good as in the shops. I just add brandy and orange to it as an alternative.' Planning way in advance, Phil had even made his Christmas pudding in May! 'That way the alcohol can really soak in!' he boasted.

On Christmas Eve, Phil took the kids out on a shopping trip. He had a few remaining ingredients to buy. Weeks before, he had ordered a turkey from the local butchers. 'I always buy my turkey from my local butchers as it tastes better than from supermarkets,' he insisted. Phil also liked to point out that it was not always necessary to buy a jumbo turkey. 'About a pound and a half pre-cooked weight (including bones) per person should be enough.'

Unlike most of the population, Phil was a real fan of turkey, but he did confess that it really tasted better the day after! 'I actually love Boxing Day food,' he claimed. 'All the leftovers from Christmas Day taste great mixed together. I love turkey hash cakes (turkey mixed with Brussels sprouts and potatoes and fried – topped with a poached egg), turkey risotto (turkey, rice, white wine, Brussels sprouts and stock), bangers 'n' mash and pork pies.'

Phil also had a few chefs' secrets up his sleeve for the Christmas dinner. Like most kids, the twins hated Brussels sprouts and Phil contested that this was probably because they had never had them cooked properly. He challenged them to test out his sprouts. He could guarantee that they would gobble up every last one on their plate. He was so certain, he even set a wager on it.

As a gesture of good will, he prepared to share his secret with the public: 'Ginger and poppy seeds go great with Brussels sprouts. No kids will really eat Brussels sprouts because they don't smell very nice. But then again, kids do eat bogeys!' But he did warn: 'The house can smell a bit after everyone has eaten lots of Brussels, though!'

Fern loved sitting down to Christmas dinner with Phil. Not only did she love his company, he was also an incredible cook! His honey parsnips and carrots were unbeatable and he also made a cheeky fruit punch, which always seemed to put guests in the Christmas spirit!

'I use good quality red wine, oranges and tea bags,' he told listeners on one radio show. 'Don't boil it, though, because it will reduce the alcohol content. Just warm it and serve in little shot glasses. I make it before the Christmas lunch and keep it in a flask!'

On Christmas Eve, Fern and Phil sat down in the living room to watch a film. That afternoon Phil had been busy making preparations for dinner the following day. ('Always spread the cooking over several days,' he advised.) Fern admired the living room. She had spent hours putting up decorations and the children loved playing with the tinsel and were mesmerised by all the fairy lights. Before bedtime, she allowed them to hang their stockings over the fireplace. Fern had even purchased a tiny stocking for baby Winnie. To Fern's relief, the children agreed to go to bed without too much protest.

By 10.00 pm the couple were both sleepy and, knowing that they had an early start the following morning, they climbed straight into bed. But it was not the thought of food that would drag them out from beneath the duvet. Phil had everything in the kitchen under control: 'My turkey goes in at 9.30 am. There is no need to get started in the oven in the middle of the night. People are scared the bird won't be cooked in time but it will.'

They expected to be woken up by Winnie, hungry for a

feed. Unfortunately, their alarm call came much earlier than expected, when she woke at 1am. Fern was exhausted, but before she had had the chance to lift her head from the pillow, Phil had climbed out of bed and was on his way to fetch Winnie. While Fern was busy breast-feeding, he ran downstairs to make a cup of tea. 'Phil's so brilliant!' she told friends. 'He'll just climb out of bed, pick up Winnie and bring up cups of tea while I feed her.'

Even though Fern and Phil always had to be up early for work, neither ever complained about their countless sleepless nights. 'It can be exhausting, but I'm not complaining,' said Fern matter-of-factly. 'That's normal family life and I'm very, very lucky. Phil's not a complainer either.' Right from the start, Phil had insisted that they share night-watch duties. 'Even if I have to be up very early, I never sleep in another room,' he proudly claimed. 'We're in this together and that's the way it is.'

Once Winnie was fast asleep, Fern and Phil drifted back into a slumber. But their peace and quiet did not last long! At around 7.00 am, Fern heard a gentle tapping on the bedroom door. She looked round to find the bedroom door slightly ajar. Three smiling little faces were staring back at her. 'Yes!' she sighed. 'You can go and get your stockings. Bring them up here and we'll open the presents together!'

'The children always climb into bed with us with their stockings from Father Christmas,' explained Fern. 'We'll open our presents downstairs and then I'll set the table with candles and crackers and Phil will start the cooking. We really are homebodies. And the best thing about Christmas will be spending time as a family.'

Although Phil discussed some of his recipes with Fern, he liked to keep most of the Christmas dinner a surprise. It was more fun that way. She had a rough idea of the dishes that he would make and without doubt she knew that they would taste phenomenal. 'Everything Phil makes will be gorgeous,' she grinned. 'And fattening!' But Fern wasn't about to start her diet on 25 December! 'That's not a problem,' she laughed. 'Christmas is no time to worry about diets. If you want a slim-line Christmas, buy a strong pair of rubber knickers!'

Ever since Phil had walked into her life, Christmas Day had become a totally new experience for Fern. For starters, she did not even have to think about the cooking! Instead, she could sit down with the kids and enjoy the day. She loved watching their faces light up as they ripped open present after present. She and Phil liked to treat the kids, but they refused to splash out on lavish gifts. Fern wanted her children to grow up with a sense of value. 'We are determined not to spoil them too much,' said Fern. 'We could ply them with the latest expensive things, but we really try not to over-indulge.'

She joked that most of her friends and family were also relieved to have Phil in the kitchen. Fern had been responsible for some disastrous Christmas dinners in her time!

'Thank goodness Phil's looking after the cooking!' she exclaimed. 'Before I did *Ready Steady Cook* mine was abysmal! People came for dinner armed with Rennies knowing it would be horrible. For pudding I'd serve up Maltesers and ice cream!'

But Phil was no saint in the kitchen. He, too, had been responsible for some culinary catastrophes in his time: 'A few years ago at the Castle Hotel in Taunton, I cooked soufflé for 120 guests at Christmas. But the oven was set at the wrong temperature, so half of them completely collapsed. Luckily, the guests were all a bit merry by then so they just thought it was funny.'

Fortunately, no such disasters occurred at Fern and Phil's own Christmas dinner. Instead, Phil cooked up an incredible feast and everyone was left feeling completely stuffed. After dinner, the children entertained guests with playful renditions of Christmas carols, while Phil dug out a few golden oldies from his record collection. Everyone agreed that it had been a thoroughly enjoyable day.

Slowly the guests trickled home, leaving Phil and Fern alone for the first time that day.

'Thanks for a wonderful meal!' said Fern, planting a kiss on Phil's cheek. 'You surpassed yourself once again!'

Phil gave a tired smile and rested his head on Fern's shoulder. 'There's something I need to show you outside,' said Fern.

'But it's freezing cold,' replied Phil. 'Can't it wait until tomorrow?'

'Not really,' begged Fern.

Reluctantly, Phil pulled on his boots and overcoat. He followed Fern out into the garage. 'What is it?' he asked, now a little confused. He had assumed that Fern was going to show him a leaking drainpipe or a loose tile on the roof that needed fixing.

'Open the garage door,' she instructed.

Still confused, Phil sighed and did as he was told. As he levered the door open, a look of shock crossed his face. In front of him was a brand new Land Rover, its bodywork glimmering in the moonlight.

'Look at the number plate,' said Fern excitedly.

Phil shone his torch downwards and read 'Merry Christmas'. He was speechless.

'Merry Christmas, darling!' said Fern. 'I'm afraid this particular present was too big for your stocking.'

'Thank you!' he finally responded. 'It's the best present I've ever been given!' He paused for a moment and corrected himself. 'Actually, it's the second-best present I've ever received.'

'What?' said Fern, slightly stunned and a little dejected. 'Well, what's the best present then?'

Phil grinned and took her in his arms. 'That's you.'

'My whole life has changed since I met Fern,' he told friends. 'Everything else takes second place. Her, Winnie and the kids are the most important things now. And Christmas is the best time of all to remember that.'

Everything in Fern's life seemed to be ticking along

nicely. Once she had ironed out the difficulties of juggling a career with motherhood, she felt much more at ease. After a few months, Winnie settled into a sleep pattern and Fern could at last get a few hours' sleep. Work on *This Morning* had also settled into a pleasant pattern. Fern loved her team and treated the studio like a second home.

One morning in October 2002, however, Fern awoke to one of the greatest shocks of her life. As she picked up the newspaper from the kitchen table, she could hardly believe her eyes. Her beloved co-host, John Leslie, was accused of being a liar and a rapist. For minutes, she sat speechless. John had become an extremely close friend over the years and Fern trusted him implicitly. She convinced herself that there must have been some terrible mistake.

Several weeks previously a furore had erupted surrounding the identity of an undisclosed rapist in former weathergirl-turned-television-presenter Ulrika Jonsson's autobiography. She claimed that a well-known celebrity had date-raped her when she was a nineteen-year-old TV-AM weathergirl, but refused to name her alleged attacker claiming that it would be his word against hers. Former *Blue Peter* host John Leslie's name emerged when his friend and fellow television presenter Matthew Wright blurted it out by mistake on his live Channel Five show *The Wright Stuff*.

He was chatting about Ulrika's claims with columnist Vivienne Parry, who claimed that two other women had approached the publicist Max Clifford with sexual allegations. 'So of the three women who we know of who have pointed the finger at John Leslie,' said Matthew Wright, 'one of them has got a book out, £16.99 in all good bookshops, the other two are working with one of the highest-profile publicists around.'

The studio fell silent. A camera then zoomed in on Vivienne. She froze in stunned silence. In an instant Matthew Wright realised his mistake and his cheeks turned crimson. In a panic, he tried to correct himself and claimed that the name-drop had been nothing more than an unfortunate slip of the tongue. He was careful not to name John Leslie again, referring instead to 'Ulrika's alleged rapist'.

At the time, John Leslie was recording *This Morning*. It was only when he left the studio at 12.30 pm that he was informed of what had happened. To make matters worse, a thrity-year-old office worker stepped up and claimed that John Leslie had also raped her in a London house three years previously.

Word spread like wildfire. Ulrika refused to comment on the accusations, issuing a statement through her lawyers, Schillings, instead, which said: 'Miss Jonsson has never named her assailant nor has she ever had any intention of doing so. Furthermore, she has never provided details from which he could be identified.'

Matthew Wright, meanwhile, was mortified by his gaffe. It was a genuine mistake, but the consequences would be tremendous. John Leslie chose to remain silent.

His agent, John Noel, merely told newspapers, 'We will not be making any comment due to legal reasons.'

Tabloids reported that earlier in the week, when John Leslie's name had been made known only to showbiz friends, he had given his own version of events. He allegedly told pals that he did have sex with Ulrika, but insisted that she had consented.

The media went into a frenzy and John Leslie went underground. There were whispers that the case would end up in court and Ulrika might even have to give evidence. Rumours were flying left, right and centre and women from all over the place were crawling out of the woodwork with a story to tell. Days after the story had broken, an additional ten women branded John Leslie a sex beast.

Bosses on *This Morning* agreed that it would be best for everyone if John took some time off. 'We have agreed with John Leslie for him to take some time off for personal reasons,' said a Granada official.

Fern was beside herself when she heard the news. John had always been a good friend and she could not believe what was happening. She rubbished the reports as nonsense and vowed to stand by him no matter what the outcome.

Pulling herself together, she made her way into the studio. On the way, she received a phone call from the production team, telling her that John would not be accompanying her that morning. What would Fern tell the viewers? She could not simply ignore the issue and pretend that nothing had happened. The popularity of

This Morning was built on trust and honesty and Fern was not about to insult the public's intelligence.

Close to tears, she sat on the sofa alone. Grave-faced, she informed viewers that John would be 'having a few days off because he has got things to sort out'. Phillip Schofield, who hosted the show on Fridays, would be stepping in as a replacement. Fern boldly told viewers: 'I am missing my partner today and he is also my friend.' She then held up a stack of supportive viewers' messages to camera and said, 'John, there are a lot of people here who love you.'

A source close to Fern gave her version of events to one newspaper. 'Obviously, Fern is very upset. She is very, very fond of John. They are close friends and Fern respects him as a broadcaster. These are very serious allegations. But that is all they are at the moment.'

Fern was the only one to stand up publicly in support of John. Friend and fellow *Blue Peter* presenter Yvette Fielding also had kind words of support. She described John as 'a lovely bloke'. She went on to say, 'It's a real shock and I'm upset. I am going to ring him. Nobody knows for sure what's going on.'

That afternoon, Fern travelled home in tears. She was a sensitive soul and her heart went out to John. She did not like to think badly of anyone, let alone her friends. But things did not get any easier. More allegations started to flood the tabloids. Reports suggested that John would be questioned by police over three separate allegations from women. Pictures of the presenter allegedly snorting cocaine had also surfaced.

A blonde PR girl claimed that John Leslie had pawed her on a racing-car simulator. She told newspapers that the incident had occurred after her marketing agency bosses had given her the job of looking after John Leslie at a family fun day. 'He was a complete arse from the moment he arrived!' she fumed. He allegedly bombarded her with sexual innuendos, before making a move.

'We brought in some simulators — the type that give you the sensation you are driving fast round a track,' she explained. 'He wanted to try one and said, "Come on, let's have a go on the stimulator. I really want to go on this stimulator. Come on." I just raised my eyes.'

'He had been making innuendos all day long and looking for double meanings for everything. I was wearing shorts and had to sit next to him. He put his hand on my knee and wouldn't take it off. He just kept squeezing for the duration of this bloody ride – about five minutes,' she said. 'I tried to laugh it off and kept telling him to move his hand. I could not believe what an idiot he was. I even pushed his hand away but he kept putting it back and I started to feel very intimidated and nervous. He must have known I was not enjoying what he was doing. He kept saying, "I'd better hold on to you because we are going so fast."'

She claimed: 'He's the sort of person that when you say, "Stop it," takes no notice. He has such a big ego and thinks it is no big deal. Since it happened I have told loads of people. Everyone is surprised because they think he is a nice telly star. But he has a real dark side.' She went on to complain, 'His status has helped him get his own way with women.'

Fern was beside herself. The following morning she did not even feel like getting out of bed, but she knew that she had a responsibility to soldier on and hold the fort while John was away. Once again, she addressed the matter on television. Looking tearful and confused, she described the situation as 'odd' and 'bewildering'.

'I expect most of you have heard, or read the newspapers yesterday, about John,' she told viewers. 'It is very bewildering for all of us and it must be bewildering for you. It is odd to read about someone you know very well in the newspapers. That's all I can say, really, except to say thank you for all your support. I honestly don't know what else to say to you, but thank you.'

She then appeared to splutter as she turned to stand-in host Phillip Schofield. Clasping his hand, she asked, 'What have we on the show today?'

But the situation only went from bad and worse. After allegations of drug taking, John Leslie's future with *This Morning* looked terribly bleak. Due to the controversy now surrounding him, Granada bosses had little option but to sack him from his £250,000-a-year presenter's job.

The allegations concerning John Leslie continued for another twelve months with both his career and life crumbling around him. In that time, he became a virtual recluse, rarely venturing out of his £2-million home in south-west London. Police investigated the many allegations made against him and eventually they amassed enough evidence to try him for assaulting a twenty-three-year-old actress.

His case was brought to trial in June 2003. But just weeks before he was due in court, it was rumoured that all charges would be dropped. According to one newspaper, Crown Prosecution Service sources had revealed that police inquiries into a string of sex accusations against the presenter had come to nothing and no charges would be brought.

Some tabloids reported that John Leslie was still furious with Ulrika Jonsson for ruining his career and was determined to seek revenge. 'He is determined to call Ulrika as a witness to prove in court that he did not attack her,' claimed one source. 'He is furious, even though Ulrika has never said anything publicly herself. He plans to ask Ulrika the truth about who raped her and he will do it in a courtroom where she cannot squirm out of answering it.'

He was also said to be preparing to sue Channel Five for identifying him as the man who allegedly raped the young weathergirl fourteen years previously.

Friends claimed that John had spent months since then compiling a dossier of evidence to establish his innocence in a High Court showdown with her. He had been collecting old phone bills and even photos. 'He believes they could prove they were still dating each other for ten weeks after the date she said the rape happened,' reported one source.

John was so convinced he would be cleared, that it was alleged he had even organised a big party to celebrate. Friends such as Fern Britton, Anthea Turner and Tim Vincent had all been invited to the champagne bash at his house and he had lined up a £550,000 deal with *OK!* magazine for his exclusive story.

But when John Leslie appeared in court in June 2003, he could not believe what happened. Sensationally he was charged with assaulting the young actress. He was accused under his real name of John Leslie Stott and gave his occupation as an actor. He was bailed to appear at London's Bow Street Magistrates on 2 July and faced a maximum jail sentence of ten years if convicted after the nine-month inquiry. His legal team was stunned and John vowed to clear his name in court.

Standing outside the Forest Gate police station in east London, dressed in a light grey suit, white shirt and blue tie, and accompanied by his girlfriend, Abi Titmuss, Leslie spoke of the anguish caused to him and his family by the investigation.

'There is absolutely no truth in the charge,' he said, trembling with anger. 'Such has been the speculation and endless rumour-mongering that I never believed that I would be able to clear my name without going through the due court process. To that extent, I eagerly await my trial to confirm my innocence and reclaim my life. Over the last nine months I have been asked to remain silent by the police and not to answer my accusers in the press in order that they could conclude their investigation quickly and without additional prejudice. I can't tell you how difficult it was for me and my family to remain silent with such accusations facing me.

'To be accused of such a crime when you are innocent is a heavy burden for any man to carry. But if you're in the media spotlight, it's a particularly cruel experience and a high price to pay for being in the public eye. This ordeal has been made all the more difficult because of how much it has upset my family, particularly my mother.

'Without their love, my girlfriend, Abi, the tremendous loyalty of my friends and supporters, this on-going nightmare would have been unbearable. I owe them everything and thank them from the bottom of my heart. I have nothing more to say. Thank you very much.'

Fern found the whole episode with John Leslie extremely upsetting. She had become very attached to him over the years and was sorry to see him go. Initially drafted in as a temporary replacement, Phillip Schofield eventually landed the plum job of being Fern's full-time co-host. Once a children's television presenter, Phillip had started his career at the BBC, where, every afternoon, he would announce the kids' programme slots from a studio affectionately known as 'the Broom Cupboard'. Gordon the Gopher, a furry hand puppet, was his popular partner in crime.

Phillip was an instant hit with the kids and went on to present the Saturday morning show *Going Live*. He would later star in a stage production of Andrew Lloyd Webber and Tim Rice's *Joseph and the Amazing Technicolor Dreamcoat*. Once famed for his boyish good looks, he had successfully made the leap from children's entertainer to adult presenter. He joked that that part of the transformation was due to an unwillingness to continue dying his hair!

Phillip and Fern quickly hit it off. Producers recognised an instant chemistry that would lure viewers in by the thousand. While they had not come together under the brightest of circumstances, it was proof that every cloud did indeed have a silver lining. Phillip had started going grey at the age of sixteen but stopped dying his hair four years previously.

'I decided to come out of the grey closet,' he said. 'Having to have it dyed every four or five weeks was such a nuisance. Also, it was becoming more fashionable to have grey hair. Richard Gere and George Clooney do, so I thought it wouldn't be such a bad club to be part of. It's funny, when you're in your twenties, it doesn't look right to have grey hair but in your forties it doesn't look right not to have grey hair.'

Both Phil and Fern shared a devilish sense of humour and could set each other off with the slightest remark. They were a true comedy double act and frequently had the studio in stitches. 'Fern is fantastic, such a professional!' said Philip in praise of his co-host. 'We both really help each other along. I do get the giggles sometimes – they call it "corpsing" in TV when you're just gripped with hysteria.'

'Fern and I are as naughty as we can get away with,' he continued. 'We were once chatting about *I'm A Celebrity...* and we made a joke about a "dry bush". It was such a smutty innuendo. But I always think you can get away with it if you say it with a smile.'

'It makes Fern laugh hysterically when someone says, "He's such a wholesome lad,"' he chuckled. 'On *This Morning* we've covered wife-swapping, orgies, sex aids and toys. There's nothing now that could embarrass me.

Very quickly, the pair became famous for their giggling fits. Often, they were uncontrollable. 'One of the worst times was in front of these twin Italian surgeons who were doing penis extentions,' explained Fern. 'Before I'd even started the link, I laughed in their faces!'

Phil recalled the incident well. 'You said something along the lines of, "Some men will go to any lengths..."' he sniggered. 'Anything that is remotely rude will make us laugh,' chuckled Fern.

After a while the production team even started to time the giggling fits! To date, their world record is for twenty-seven seconds! 'That was for beef dunking!' nodded Phil. 'We had a couple who had written a book about dunking biscuits, and I said that I didn't like it. Then, later on, we had some beautiful roast beef and I cut a piece and dipped it in some mustard. Fern said, "Ah, so you don't mind dunking a bit of beef?" We were uncontrollable and had to go to an ad break after twenty-seven seconds because we realised there was no chance of recovery!'

The fits became so frequent, that at one point the crew decided to install a red panic button. 'If things did get uncontrollable we could press it and the crew would know we were in trouble,' explained Fern. 'That kept us sane for a while, but now it's disappeared we're insane again.'

By all accounts, Phillip had been Fern's downfall. 'I used to pride myself that I'd never corpsed on TV,' she said, shaking her head. 'But when I got together with Phillip that all went out of the window.'

On the outside, Fern and Phil appeared to be such a wholesome pair, but together they had a very bad streak. People were often surprised to discover that they had a 'naughty side'. Their work on *This Morning* brought them into contact with all sorts of weird and wonderful characters. 'We know more about all kinds of extraordinary activities that people would be shocked about!' declared Fern.

'I couldn't imagine anything could shock me now!' added Phillip. 'But it's all bums and willies that make me laugh the most!' giggled Fern.

Fern recalled the most shocking story they had ever covered on the show. 'There was this poor woman who smoked too much and her circulation stopped working.

And when she was walking around the lounge, she brushed against a cushion and her fingers fell off!' Even retelling the story caused Fern to erupt into fits of giggles.

'That surprised me!' continued Phil. 'She couldn't even pick her fingers up. Then she got so fed up when one of her fingers wouldn't fall off, she took the electric carving knife to it. And they were her smoking fingers.'

Fern continued the story. 'After that her husband smoked for her. He would hold her cigarettes up to her mouth. And she claims her problems weren't due to smoking!'

Another amusing incident involved a guest who claimed that she could have orgasms every thirty seconds. Phillip turned to her and said, 'So you're obviously having one now?' She replied, 'Yes, yes... and that was another one!'

'We also had a woman who was a forty-year-old virgin, and we discussed in the morning if we would be able to spot her when she came into the studio,' recalled Phillip. 'Then this lady walked in and we looked at each other and went, "Forty-year-old virgin."' After that, Phil and Fern completely lost their composure. The studio floor manager even had to step in and take the pair outside! 'We were told to get it out of our system and then go and do the item,' smiled Fern.

'We're not very good with funny names either!' confessed Phillip. 'I think the show purposefully books people with funny names. We had a Mr and Mrs Nob on the show once.' Fern had a few suggestions of her own: 'And there was a surgeon who specialised in bladder problems – he was called Mr Tinkle. And if people talk in a funny voice, that finishes us off as well!'

Not everyone on the show was quite so interesting, however; Fern and Phillip had both interviewed their fair share of dull celebrities. 'At times Fern and I have interviewed people and they've been so dull we've almost said, "Do you have any questions you want to ask us?"' confessed Phillip. 'Or I'll be so bored I find myself watching one of the boats floating by instead. I wouldn't name names, though.'

It was obvious that both Phil and Fern were good pals. Their on-and-off screen capers made going to work less of a chore and more of a social event. Fern would tenderly refer to Phillip as 'Pip', while Phillip struck upon the nickname 'Minty' for Fern. He coined the name after Fern told viewers that she had accidentally splattered her nightie with mint sauce: 'I was in my nightie and reached to the top shelf and a bottle of mint sauce smashed all over the place! You've no idea how far mint sauce goes. It went up the opposite wall and up my nightie – a long way up.'

The joke continued for quite some time and former pop singer Kerry McFadden even presented Fern with a huge pair of knickers bearing the nickname 'Minty' when she appeared as a guest on the show.

While Fern loved her co-host dearly, she was not averse to the odd burst of violent behaviour – as Phillip would find out the painful way! The pair were changing positions as they prepared to introduce a competition when Fern suddenly smacked him between the legs and giggled: 'I've just hit you in an area, haven't I?' Phillip then groaned, 'Yeah,' and put on a high-pitched voice to say, 'I'm all right.' But show insiders said he needed to sit down and recover once the show had finished. 'Phillip had the wind taken out of him but he's forgiven Fern for her flying fists,' reported one source.

Aside from that isolated incident, however, Fern and Phillip got on like a house on fire. Whenever the occasion arose, they were happy to socialise with each other off-set. 'Our social events are disgraceful!' giggled Fern, with a sly wink. 'We drink a lot, eat very little, spend an enormous amount of money and go home hungry and pissed.'

The pair was asked to present the British Soap Awards in 2006 and could not wait to get stuck into the after-show party! They already had outfits planned. 'I'm wearing something from a couple of very young designers. They're called something like... "I'll feel you up!"' she joked, before correcting herself. 'No, its Orphelia Fancy! It's a bit like the kind of dress the queen in *Snow White* would wear.' As for Phlilip, he preferred to stick with a dinner jacket.

'I think we are going to be on our best behaviour, though!' he promised. 'It's the biggest awards night going so it's very exciting.' Fern was also excited: 'I'm such a soap fiend! I'll love it. I can't wait to stand in the same room as all these people that I love watching.'

Phillip had the utmost respect for his leading lady. She

was by far his favourite 'work wife' to date. 'Fern's a sexy girl,' he said. 'I think it's because she's very cheeky and she knows it. I'd definitely fancy her over Kate Moss because you want someone real. I'm attracted to people who can throw their head back and laugh. Fern is one of those people and my wife is another. She's honest, sexy, sensitive and filthy. What more could you ask for in a woman?'

But Phillip's wife, Stephanie, had nothing to worry about!

'I know how lucky I am to have found Steph,' admitted Phillip. 'She's perfect for me. She's a great mate, a great wife and a great mum. I'm very secure in my marriage. We sat up at the end of the garden under the weeping willow last night because it was so hot and drank glasses of champagne. We still make each other laugh.'

Stephanie had no reason whatsoever to be jealous of Fern. 'She's got the confidence to know there's nothing to it,' Phil maintained. 'And we all get on well as a foursome – me, my wife, Fern and her husband, Phil Vickery. We have outrageous afternoons where we drink lots of expensive alcohol and then get a car home and fall out of it at the other end.'

Phillip was not the only man who considered Fern sexy. By now, she had quite a following of male admirers. Whole Internet sites had been dedicated to her ample bosom. 'It's all about my tits and things, isn't it?' she would joke. 'You know, I am what I am. I didn't always look like this, but now I do. I keep as fit as I can be but nothing seems to happen. You just have to get on with life.

As long as my husband and my kids are happy, that's fine.'

However, one fan even went so far as to send Fern sexy underwear in the mail. Fern revealed that every birthday and Christmas she was sent black silk stockings by a navy officer admirer. She was amazed by how 'perfectly packaged' they always arrived. But Phillip's fans had gone one step further. He was once sent an envelope stuffed with pubic hair! 'I do get fan mail, but the weirdest thing was when a woman sent me an envelope full of her pubic hairs,' he laughed. 'She'd shaved it all off for me. But when I opened it in the office it made everyone jump, so I don't think it had the desired effect.'

Fern managed to send the male population into a frenzy when she agreed to pose for some raunchy calendar shots. Draped on a *chaise longue* with just a velvet wrap to cover her modesty, she was photographed for the *This Morning Exposed* charity calendar. Not wanting to miss out, her husband Phil also lent his services to the project. Perched on a worktop he had only an apron to conceal himself.

Clearly discovering a taste for this naked modelling lark, Phil went on to pose for another calendar. This time it was for the women's magazine *Cosmopolitan*. 'It was for prostate cancer and a friend of mine died of it so I was very up for it,' he explained. 'I don't exercise really so I'm quite lucky that I'm not bigger and was in good shape. Me, Pat Cash and Gary Rhodes were all at the same photoshoot for the magazine. Gary Rhodes was quite porky then but he saw me and I think that's why he toned up.'

In fact, over the past couple of years Phil had emerged from Fern's shadow and had quite a discernable following of his own. 'Someone actually ran the idea past me to go onto *I'm A Celebrity...* this year,' he revealed. 'I'd like to do it because I'd like to eat lots of weird food. I'd love to catch a snake and eat it.'

'I bet you wouldn't!' teased Fern.

'I'd eat a kangaroo's penis no problem. I've eaten a bull's ball before and locusts!' he boasted. Eventually, however, the producers decided Phil wasn't right for the show: 'In the end people said I was too macho for the show and they needed someone a bit more wimpy!'

But Phil did have a secret penchant for reality television shows. 'I'd love to do a *Hell's Kitchen*-type programme but I would be nice and use convenience foods. [Former *Brookside* actress] Jennifer Ellison was good. I'd want it to be relaxed – but I'd be quite bossy, though. Gordon Ramsay's great but there is a competitiveness between all the TV chefs, which I try to keep out of!' So who was his favourite chef, then? 'Nigella Lawson is gorgeous. Very beautiful indeed. You look at her and you just think, "Wow!" She's done very well!'

Both in business and at home, Phil and Fern were an extremely successful couple. While John Leslie's court case had overshadowed the early part of Fern's career on *This Morning*, she had since forged a wonderful professional relationship with her second Phil, Mr Schofield. It had taken some time, but Fern Britton was finally on course for a balanced life. Absolutely nothing could stand in her way now.

Chapter 12

Having her Cake and Eating it!

In January 2006, British women shunned the likes of Victoria Beckham and Madonna to name cuddly Fern Britton as the celebrity that they would most like to be, in a poll commissioned by Boots. The *X Factor* judge Sharon Osbourne trailed behind in second place.

When Fern's agent called her up with the news, she was dumbstruck. 'When they told me I thought, "Are you taking the mickey?"' she said incredulously. 'It's hilarious. It's one of those things that's terribly nice but makes you slightly embarrassed. Also, you don't think it's quite true.'

Fern considered herself to be in a completely different league to the likes of Posh Spice. She simply was not that kind of celebrity. 'But I wouldn't mind wearing big diamonds and going out to lunch,' she pondered. 'And I wouldn't mind a figure like hers either. But I wouldn't like to have the spotlight on my marriage like that. It's horrible to have your personal life on the front pages.'

Several months later, Fern came up tops in a second poll, beating the likes of Kelly Brook and Posh Spice, to be named the UK's 'most beddable' star. Bosses at *This Morning* even threw a celebratory barbeque in her honour. Fern happily tucked into burgers and hot dogs, not giving a second thought to her waistline.

Since starting work on *This Morning*, Fern's profile had been raised dramatically.

'I don't understand that either!' she said, stunned, 'because I spend my life trying to be as low profile as possible. At home, I usually look appalling. My favourite outfit is a pair of very old Marks & Spencer training bottoms, which I roll up attractively to my knees and wear with sheepskin boots, plus a T-shirt, which is usually filthy after the children have thrown spaghetti bolognese at me.' There were certainly no airs and graces in the Britton–Vickery household: 'I'll have no make-up on and my hair will be standing on end,' continued Fern, with classic self-deprecation. 'My mother goes mad – she's utterly attractive and perfectly groomed. I'm just not!'

On plenty of occasions, Phil had joked that he was in fact married to two different women: one was a glamorous television presenter and the other an earthy woman who does not wear make-up. He said, 'When I'm working at home, I have the telly on in the kitchen. I look at this woman presenting *This Morning* and think, "Cor, she's sexy." Then she comes home, takes her make-up off and it's like having two women in my life.'

It was Fern's ability to swing between sexy, well-heeled television celebrity and down-to-earth, loving mum that made her such a hit with fans. Many had grown up with Fern, tracking her career through various newsrooms. She made a point of keeping in touch with those long-term fans. Fern knew her career would be nothing without their support. 'Children started writing to me when I first appeared on television and a couple of them have kept in touch throughout the intervening twenty-one years,' she smiled. 'I always reply to fan letters.'

While Fern was often baffled by her popularity, Phil found her appeal obvious. 'Someone wrote that Fern is a national icon, which is very nice,' he explained. 'I've never met anybody who doesn't like her. What you see is what you get. Whether she's on telly or at Marks & Spencer, she'll stop and have a chat with you.'

Fern was not sure about the tag 'national icon', but she would humorously refer to herself as a 'national landmark'. Her willingness to talk openly and candidly about her weight instantly made women up and down the country warm to her. She was large but sexy and proud of her figure. Plus, there was absolutely nothing threatening about Fern; she could put anyone at ease. Fern would regularly confess her weight hang-ups on air. Viewers admired her for refusing to adhere to super-slim stereotypes, preferring instead to celebrate her natural body shape.

'Let's face it. I would have to do a lot of work if I wanted to end up looking like Demi Moore!' she chuckled. 'So I just have to think that anything I can do for myself is a positive – no matter how little.'

Fern was proud of her body. Over the years she had learned to love what society deemed to be imperfections. 'I'm a voluptuous size sixteen and proud of it!' she exclaimed. 'Of course I want to wake up tomorrow a size ten, but it doesn't work that way.'

Whenever Fern's name was mentioned in the press, it was usually in the context of weight gain and dieting. As long as the message was positive, Fern was not too bothered. She was fully aware that much of her appeal was down to the fact that she presented an attainable image. She was not some stick-thin Hollywood celebrity a million miles removed from the grit and grime of everyday life.

'I would be the first to admit that the viewers wouldn't relate to me as well if I was a size eight and had no lines on my face,' she admitted. 'This face has lived and I'm actually quite proud of that. It says I am a survivor.'

Besides, Fern barely had enough time to splash her face with cold water let alone indulge herself in time-consuming beauty treatments. As she said, 'There are these women who put great emphasis on looking after themselves, having facials and getting their legs waxed and going to the gym and popping along for their Botox injections. It's just not me! I can't help but feel that if you are spending all that time on your looks, you are missing out on other things. All these women who have little nips and tucks and sit for an hour and a half having their nails stuck on – it's such a waste of time!'

'I believe women of my age obsessed with looking perfect are unhappy in other areas of their lives,' she continued. 'They must be so self-obsessed that they don't have much real life. I have so much real life. I don't have time to be self-obsessed. I know that if I had to run off for beauty appointments every week, my children would be missing out. I used to love booking myself into a health farm for a bit of pampering but those days are gone. The most I do now is get my hair done!'

Of course, Fern would love to have more time for pampering, but as a mother with a hectic work schedule, it simply was not possible. 'Pampering is my idea of heaven!' she confessed. 'If only I had the time. Instead, it would be: "Could you hurry up with that back massage, please. I've got to be out in ten minutes..."'

Fern was happy to grow old gracefully: 'Getting old doesn't worry me. Being a bit larger doesn't worry me. I'm not twenty any more and I've accepted that.'

Fern had no qualms about showing off her curves in public. She even revealed to viewers on live television that she had accidentally flashed her boobs at a neighbour. 'Something very embarrassing happened to me yesterday,' she giggled. 'I had been in the garden all day as it was so beautiful. When it was bath-time for my two-year-old daughter, I said, "I'm going to get in with you." So I was completely naked and then I thought, "I'll just close the sash window" – bearing in mind it's 5pm so the sun's shining! I got to the window and it's a bit sticky and I'm pushing against the glass – but we share a drive with a neighbour and she drove in. She saw me and waved. You have never seen someone move so fast behind the curtain. I immediately looked in the mirror to check what she'd seen.'

'Was it like the three of spades?' asked Philip Schofield, bursting into a fit of laughter.

Fern then turned to the camera and apologised to her neighbour. 'I'm so sorry I embarrassed yourself and me.'

Even though Fern could laugh at herself, deep down she was proud of her sexy body. At one point, she had even considered having a risqué tattoo on her bottom. 'I was going to get a little cherub on my bum,' she revealed. 'Luckily, the shop was closed, so I'll never know if I would have had the courage to go through with it!' she confessed.

What disgusted Fern was not her actual weight, but people's attitude towards it. She had always had a particular bugbear with snooty designer shops unwilling to accommodate the larger woman: 'I don't shop in posh shops – partly because nothing fits me and partly because I can't bear the attitude that if you aren't a size eight, you're a second-class citizen.'

Fern recalled an especially humiliating incident. She was out shopping with Phil at the time, in search of an outfit for a party. Noticing a pretty dress in the window, she walked into one designer shop. Glancing through several items on the clothes rail, she noticed a shop assistant creeping up behind her. 'Nothing for you today, dear,' said the woman condescendingly. 'You must be disappointed.'

Fern was furious. 'Well, perhaps stores like this should think about catering for people like me!' she exclaimed, the anger rising in her throat.

'Have you thought of losing half a stone?' the woman replied.

Fern couldn't believe the woman's audacity! Phil practically had to drag Fern out of the shop kicking and screaming. 'I wanted to punch her!' Fern fumed.

Fern was sick and tired of being made to feel like a leper. Why should she feel embarrassed about her body? Equally, she hated the sympathy vote. 'You can tell there are people watching me and thinking, "Oh, the poor tubby woman must go home and sob her heart out over her size,"' she said. 'But it's just not true.'

She also recalled an incident at her kids' school gates. Another parent had approached her with what he thought was a flattering compliment. 'My wife really admires you,' he said earnestly. 'You know, for looking the way you do.' Fern was left speechless. Why couldn't she just be happy with the way she was?

In a fit of defiance she decided that it was time to let it all hang out. It was the height of summer in 2005 and Fern and Phil were planning their annual family holiday to Constantine Bay in Cornwall. They rented a caravan in a holiday park every year. Fern describes it as 'her favourite place in the world.... The kids adore it!'

Despite being one of the best-paid presenters on television, Fern shunned expensive holidays in favour of a good, old-fashioned, British break. She had never been a fan of exotic holidays: 'I don't see home enough as I'm in the studio so often.'

Fern, Phil and the kids loved returning to the same spot each year. They were friendly with all the locals and often had friends from London come to visit. On one holiday, the celebrity chef Gordon Ramsey even popped down. Unfortunately and rather embarrassingly, his £100,000 car broke down on the way home and Phil had to go and help him jump-start it, much to Fern's amusement.

Busy making preparations for the holiday, Fern had a free afternoon and decided to grab some last-minute bits and bobs from the shops. She specifically needed something to wear on the beach. Usually she opted for a black swimsuit, supposedly the most flattering option for a larger woman. 'Why don't you go for a bikini this year?' winked Phil. Fern thought for a moment. 'Why not?' she smiled. What on earth was she hiding from?

'This year I thought, "No. No swimsuits for me. Bikini,"' she proudly declared. 'And I bought a bikini.' Fern opted for a black number, 'with proper bra support and nice shaped pants'. When she returned home to show Phil, he demanded a private fashion show. Fern could not wait to wear it out on the beach. 'And do you know?' she grinned. 'No one was sick on the beach. No one recoiled in horror!'

Grace would run up to Fern and wrap her little arms around her mummy's belly. 'They'd come up to me and wobble my tummy and go, "You've got a very wobbly tummy,"' laughed Fern. 'And I'd say, "Yes, I've got a very wobbly tummy."'

Next, Grace would grab Fern's breasts. 'You've got very wobbly bosoms,' Grace would exclaim. 'Yes, I have got very wobbly bosoms,' said Fern, shaking her head. 'There, I'm sorry about that, but that's it.'

In actual fact, Fern's kids loved her cuddly figure. Fern said, 'My daughter Grace says, "I don't want you to be thin," and all the kids like to bounce on my tummy and rest their heads on my bosom.'

Fern would rather her kids remembered her as fat and happy rather than thin and miserable. 'Do I want my kids to see me moping around depressed or frustrated?' she asked. 'Wouldn't it be better to be remembered as a jolly old soul?'

But while Fern relaxed on holiday, a media storm brewed back home. Pictures of Fern in her bikini had made the national papers and they sparked a major debate about weight issues. The morning after the pictures were published, Fern appeared on *This Morning* and laughed off her rather tubby appearance. Instead, she showed viewers what she thought to be more realistic holiday snaps.

Many women's magazines came out in support of Fern,

commending her bravery and confidence. Others, however, criticised Fern for promoting an unhealthy lifestyle. They also picked up on several comments that Fern had made about dieting: 'Diets? I hate them! If diets worked we'd all look like Carol Vorderman and be a size eight.' She allegedly told one magazine that she had tried a series of low-calorie regimes and no longer cared that she was overweight. 'Most of it is so boring and life is so short. I like my roast dinners and my husband likes his. What is sexy anyway? To me it's about having charisma, not a great bum. This figure is the only one I've got, so I'd better get on with it.'

The nutritionist Nora Lane, of the nationwide slimming club Vitaline, was one of the many to voice their concerns. 'Fern is being highly irresponsible by coming out with this nonsense,' she said. 'She should not promote opinions that are clearly wrong and positively dangerous. She's in the public eye and should set an example to her fans. If she has given up on losing weight that is her mistake, but she should not promote the idea.'

'Properly balanced diets do not have to be boring,' she continued. 'Everybody can be healthy, attain a reasonable weight – and enjoy their food – if they combine healthy eating with exercise. Fern may claim to be happy now but as she gets older she will almost certainly suffer ill health directly as a result of being overweight.

'The large number of overweight people in this country is the largest single burden on the NHS. Thirty per cent of the British population is obese, and all are at risk of serious illness as a result. Her opinions are not only wrong, they are potentially harmful. It is obesity not dieting that has been directly linked with depression. People watching her programme may have an undiagnosed serious condition like diabetes and after listening to her decide to just eat what they like. Fern is talking dangerous nonsense and a person in her position of influence should refrain from doing so.'

Other newspapers followed suit with similar criticisms. 'Three-quarters of adults are overweight and the number of Britons classed as obese has quadrupled in the past twenty-five years to a staggering 30 per cent,' claimed one. 'Obesity-related illnesses cost the NHS £500 million each year – a third of the amount spent on diseases linked to smoking – not to mention the £2 billion it is estimated to cost the economy in terms of lost productivity. It plays a part in 30,000 deaths every year. And every reputable doctor warns that these figures are set to soar in the years ahead.'

Fern did confess that doctors had warned her to shed a few pounds. 'Medical experts are telling me I'm cutting my life short and with a young family, that's pretty terrifying,' she admitted. But she hit back at claims that she was promoting an unhealthy lifestyle. Just because she refused to follow low-calorie diet plans did not mean that she lived on junk. She ate well and exercised regularly.

'The people writing these things don't know me. You

don't know what I eat, you don't know how hard I'm trying to keep in shape,' she told viewers on *This Morning*. 'On this show we promote health and wellbeing and that is what I believe in.'

'I am forty-eight, I have four children, I am a working mother,' she continued. 'Where is fitness on your list of priorities? Right down the bottom – just like me.' But she did point out that she was keen to be healthier for her family's sake. 'I don't wish to die early and leave my children motherless. I'm not about to drop off the perch just yet!'

Although she did not like to make too much of a fuss in public, Fern was deeply hurt by the criticism. It might not seem obvious to others, but Fern was a very vulnerable person. 'I'm too trusting,' she sighed. 'I get hurt very easily and find out the hard way that people think I am a walk-over. Phil tells me I am much too soft.

'What hurt me was the attendant stuff where somebody made up an interview claiming that I said diets are rubbish and I don't care about my health. That was made up, it's not what I believe in at all. I try to be fit and I've always been active.'

Of course, being with Phil had helped boost her confidence, as she noted, 'Having someone you can be completely honest with, who is always by your side, is just so reassuring.'

Phil supported Fern in her claim that fad diets were pointless. 'Crazy diets wind me up,' he fumed. 'I think

Gwyneth Paltrow, for example, has to be very careful with her macrobiotic diet. As I'm mainly a pastry chef, my brother, who is a doctor, gives me some stick about some of the stuff I make. However, I believe there is no such thing as an evil food – it is how much you eat. You can have every food in moderation. The only diet I like is a balanced diet. I will quite happily give my kids sugar, Coke and burgers. There is nothing wrong with alcohol – providing you don't drink nine pints a night.'

Determined to prove she was serious about fitness, Fern signed up for a number of sporting activities. She had always been a fan of Pilates. 'I do it on the bathroom floor at 5.15 am every morning for fifteen minutes before going to work,' she claimed. 'I'm hardly what you'd call toned, but I think that any exercise you can do is a positive thing.'

After hearing of her interest, a production team approached Fern with the idea of releasing a fitness video. With so many celebrity-endorsed videos on the market, it made sense to have one featuring a personality to whom normal women could relate. Fern recorded the video *Lynne Robinson's Everyday Pilates With Fern Britton* with the assistance of Pilates expert Lynne Robinson. It featured short workouts designed to suit a busy lifestyle. 'I don't have much time to spend on myself, and this video was made for busy women like me,' explained Fern.

She also signed up to take part in a charity bike ride in autumn 2005. 'I've always liked cycling,' she explained. 'I'm cycling madly at the moment, because I'm doing a big charity bike ride in November,' she said proudly. 'I'm going to cycle along the Nile with 200 other women. I love being at work, I love being at home, but I wanted something else that was for me. I can do fifty miles, no problem, and I've stopped drinking – but have I lost an ounce? No. I've put half a stone on!'

Fern's second bike ride took place in Rajasthan in November 2006. She pedalled 250 miles for the Women For Women Appeal. The ride certainly turned out to be a memorable experience!

'The first day was really tough as I had two punctures and my chain came off three times,' she reported back. But there was worse to come. After cycling through rural villages, Fern was left soaked in raw sewage! 'All the effluent is poured into the middle of the road in the rural areas we ride through and we're all covered in poop soup! The worst thing is that we can only wash it off with buckets of water before we get to the place where we stay at night.'

Soon after completing the race, Fern was sent to Buckingham Palace to conduct an interview with Prince Edward Earl of Wessex. Making idle chit-chat, she told him about the race. 'Do you know, at one stage I had two pairs of cycling shorts on with padding. It was so bad.' She suddenly paused before adding, 'Sorry, I don't know why I'm discussing my bottom with you. It was tender, let's put it like that.'

A grinning Prince Edward replied: 'I'm surprised you're sitting down, then.'

It was Fern's ability to keep the same tone with royalty and members of the general public alike that made her such a refreshing celebrity.

Proving that fitness did play an important role in her lifestyle, Fern defied the critics. She was even invited to present a new show for ITV1 called *Looking Good, Feeling Great*. She accepted, but though she was prepared to up her exercise regime, Fern drew the line at going to the gym. 'You're joking!' she laughed. 'I run up and down the stairs 17,000 times in an evening. I've done quite a lot of Pilates and yoga, but I'm having to take a bit of a break from that because I simply don't have time. It's hopeless!'

Phil also helped Fern come up with a practical, but tasty, eating plan, as Fern explained, 'You do what you can because you live a very chaotic lifestyle. You eat breakfast and lunch where you can get it, and when I get home I'm starving, so I might make the wrong choices. I eat good food, but perhaps not at the right time or in the right quantities. It's not that I don't believe in dieting – I'm tempted all the time not to eat, not to drink, to exercise. But I don't seem to get round to doing it!'

Fern had her own theories on looking good and feeling great. It was not all about dieting and exercise. 'Try and look after yourself, but don't think about yourself too much,' she advised. 'There's no point worrying about everything. Keep life simple. You can't be happy all of the time. You just have to do your best and enjoy it. If you're not enjoying something, stop it. If you're in an unhappy marriage or you're not happy at work or you're fed up with what's happening to you, then walk away. It's destructive to every part of you, your self-esteem and everything else. There's always a way out.'

Not everyone considered Fern's weight to be a problem. She clearly led a healthy lifestyle and was a positive role model for the average working mother. When marketing directors for the health food brand Ryvita were searching for a celebrity to front their latest advertising campaign, Fern seemed the obvious choice!

They approached her agent with the idea. In the advert, Fern would be eating a packet of Ryvita Minis in her dressing room with her head superimposed on the body of a skinny woman. Someone from the wardrobe department would then come in and give her a fat suit to put on before going off to present a television show. Fern roared with laughter when she heard the idea; she thought it was hilarious! 'I love the joke!' she insisted. 'I don't mind laughing at myself. I'm not always confident but once you get past forty you think to yourself: "I'm not going to take any crap from anybody." You see people wasting their lives looking in the mirror, worrying about every wrinkle. Well, you're going to look worse in ten years' time, so you might as well enjoy the way you are now.'

'Fern was the perfect choice for the tongue-in-cheek adverts,' said Ryvita's marketing director Rob Murray. 'Like our consumers, she doesn't take herself too seriously and appreciates life is too short to worry about dieting all the time.'

Fern had a riot filming the advert. While getting ready in her dressing room, she gave a cheeky two-finger salute to the super-slim model cast as her body double. 'If only!' she joked to the crew. An exact replica of her body – complete with ample breasts and mummy tummy – had been created from latex. When somebody accidentally referred to it as a 'fat suit' Fern shrieked with laughter.

When the adverts finally aired there were inevitably several complaints. Watchdogs accused the brand of promoting a 'bad body image'. Fern shrugged off the complaints. Most people found them as they were intended – humorous and light-hearted.

In 2007, Fern appeared in a second series of adverts for Ryvita. This time she was cast in a series of different guises with the help of camera trickery. First, she appeared as an eight-year-old schoolgirl, posing with pigtails and a crispbread in her hand. She then morphed into a double-jointed yoga freak and a Geordie brickie with a hard hat. Finally, she appeared as herself, her face splattered with mashed fruit after trying to blend berries. Once again the adverts were an instant hit.

The public loved Fern Britton. Even her harshest critics found it difficult to fault the woman! By day she was a successful television personality, but after hours she was a full-time mum and wife. She experienced the same highs, lows and struggles as every other human being. But unlike most celebrities, Fern was willing to discuss her experiences openly and share them with the public. She was everyone's best friend.

Fern had never set out to be a successful television celebrity, yet she had ended up one of the highest-paid presenters in the UK. She had to admit it had all happened by accident! Fern loved her job dearly, but if it all fell apart tomorrow she would not really worry. Family had always been her main priority. No matter how much fun she had had in the studio that day, Fern could not wait to get home and snuggle on the sofa with Phil and the kids. That was real life.

Admittedly, her life was not perfect, but she had learned to accept the things about herself that she could not change and to change the things she could. She had never expected instant results; it was an ongoing process, as she said: 'It's no secret that I would like to get more balance in my life and have more time with the children.'

Thanks mainly to Phil's love and support – along with excellent medical care – Fern could now control her bouts of depression. She did, however, suffer the occasional twinge. 'Sometimes I'm really stressed out,' she confessed. 'Then I hit the wall and have to go to bed.' Under doctor's orders, she was now on a mild course of HRT (hormone replacement therapy). Feeling confused, aggressive and 'a bit hotter than you should be,' she had taken a blood test. 'It's lovely,' she said of the treatment. 'I find I'm not snappy at the children. My son Harry said to me the other day, "What are those pills you're taking? I've noticed you're a lot nicer."'

Real life was great, but it wasn't easy. Ultimately, however, Fern was blissfully happy. Her desires in life were quite simple: 'I want to go to bed knowing I have done as much as possible so that I don't open the kitchen door in the morning and have it all avalanche down on me. At the end of the day, if the sink is wiped and the rubbish is out, I'm quite happy.'

'I'm a very lucky person and I've got a very lovely job and I'm happier now than I've ever, ever been,' she confessed. 'But I'm just a normal woman, trying to scrape the burnt spaghetti hoops off the bottom of the pan. After all, we are supposed to be fab mothers, great at our jobs and still have plenty of loo rolls in the house!'